Sidelines
and Bloodlines

Sidelines and Bloodlines

A Father, His Sons, and Our Life in College Football

Ryan McGee
with Dr. Jerry E. McGee
and Sam McGee

TRIUMPH
BOOKS

Library of Congress Cataloging-in-Publication Data available upon request.

This book is available in quantity at special discounts for your group or organization. For further information, contact:
Triumph Books LLC
814 North Franklin Street
Chicago, Illinois 60610
(312) 337-0747
www.triumphbooks.com

Printed in U.S.A.

ISBN: 978-1-62937-787-2

Design by Nord Compo

Photos courtesy of McGee family collection unless otherwise indicated

CONTENTS

FOREWORD

I N THE SUMMER OF 1997, just a couple years into my tenure at ESPN, I got a call from one of our executives. He said, "We'd like you to host the weekend version of *RPM2Night.*" It was a nightly show on still-new ESPN2 dedicated entirely to motorsports.

Now, in the minds of those who make such decisions, this probably made perfect sense. *Hey, Rece is from Alabama. He probably loves motorsports!* At least, that's what I imagine they thought. It didn't make as much sense to me. First, I was hosting *NBA2Night* and I had just been the studio host for the NBA Finals on ESPN Radio. That role gave me an elevated courtside view of the Michael Jordan "Flu Game." I was working with play-by-play legend Brent Musburger and ESPN legend Dan Patrick, who was covering the Finals for *SportsCenter.* I was having a blast. My primary ambition was plotting how to parlay the NBA hosting role into working on the sport I'd grown up loving most, college football.

So, I replied to the executive on the other end of the line, "If you're thinking, 'Hey, let's get the Southern guy to do the car racing show,' then you've got the wrong dude. Don't get me wrong; I know the show is important, and I'll work my tail off to learn it. But I have to tell you that I only have a functional knowledge of the sport." I knew that Jeff Gordon drove car No. 24, Dale Earnhardt was No. 3, and Rusty Wallace was No. 2. That's about it. They wanted me to take the host role anyway. Becoming the weekend host of *RPM2Night* was how I met Ryan McGee.

Ryan was a production assistant on the show and a rising star. He had great vision and insight for television production. He was patient and helpful while I got my racing knowledge up to speed. When he brought me a shot sheet (the script page an anchor uses to describe the highlight) or a story idea, he included plenty of extra detail to help me along. Maybe he did that for everyone, but he probably felt an obligation considering we were among the very few Southerners working in Bristol. Ryan claims we were the only two. We were definitely the only two who fully appreciated real sweet tea (you can't just add sugar after it's brewed) and the Third Saturday in October, between his Vols and my Crimson Tide.

Even if we bled different shades in the Alabama-Tennessee rivalry, there was a near-instant bond. For Ryan and me, there was a kinship that transcended allegiance to our alma maters. It was a similar deep appreciation for how college football becomes almost like strands of our DNA. Ryan's college football DNA extends a little past that of a typical fan, given that his father, Jerry, was one of the top game officials in the sport.

Ryan's passion is not an irrationally rabid, paint-your-face, hate-every-wretched-breath-a-rival-sucks-into-his-greedy-lungs, smash-your-television, and tweet-"fire-the-coach"-after-every-loss fervor. It's understanding how that sometimes over-the-top zeal dovetails with and mysteriously reflects the more rational deep devotion to the sport, and how it makes college football unique among all sports in America.

In 2019, we worked together on ESPN's College Football 150 project titled *The Greatest*, in which we ranked every-thing—the top players, coaches, mascots, stadiums, moments, and everything in between. Ryan's extraordinary grasp of why college football is so ingrained in our culture was evident. It wasn't just knowing the stories. He has an uncanny ability to share them in a way that connects with people.

I'm also proud to be a small part of Ryan's most important connection. We were still on the racing beat in 1998 when Ryan told me he wanted to propose to his girlfriend, Erica. But it had been a long-distance romance for a while, and his ring funds had taken a hit by going to visit her. I told him I knew a guy who could help. My father-in-law was in the jewelry business and helped Ryan expedite the engagement.

Twenty years later, I finally got a good look at the ring when our families ran into each other at Walt Disney World. He recounted the ring story to my wife with the warmth, sincerity, and self-effacing humor that are his trademarks as a reporter and a writer. Those qualities are captured perfectly as Ryan shares how college football has provided celebration and solace in *Sidelines and Bloodlines: A Father, His Sons, and Our Life in College Football.*

—**Rece Davis** *is the host of* College GameDay, *ESPN's flagship college football program. He also hosts the network's on-site coverage of the College Football Playoff and has been a regular contributor to* SportsCenter *and other ESPN shows and platforms since he joined the network in 1995.*

PROLOGUE

ONE LAST TIME...
FOR REAL THIS TIME

2009 BCS National Championship
Coral Gables, Florida
January 8, 2009

"YOU THINK WE CAN GET them to slow that clock down?"

My father spoke to me in a conversational, almost quiet tone. Well, as quiet and conversational as one can be while talking on the sideline of a football stadium surrounded by 78,466 other people. The game clock was ticking toward 00:00 in the 2009 BCS National Championship Game. To everyone else in the nation, that countdown was moving toward the end of college football's 139th season and the coronation of the Florida Gators as champions, entering the final minutes of icing a 24–14 home-state victory over the Oklahoma Sooners.

But for four of us there in Dolphin Stadium that night, the end of the game meant the end of the officiating career of my father, Dr. Jerry Edward McGee, also known as the gray-haired guy with the big white "F" on the back of his black-and-white-striped jersey. After 404 college football games, 300 at the sport's highest level, this one—the biggest one he'd ever worked—was going to be it.

Or so he'd promised. For real this time.

Dad's officiating career had included two Rose Bowls, a pair of Army-Navy games, and two dozen postseason contests in all. Three of those games, including this one, had determined the national championship. But before this night on this stage, there had been much smaller games played in much smaller venues under much dimmer lights and under the gaze of exactly zero TV cameras. The first time he'd stepped onto a collegiate football field with a whistle was nearly 37 years earlier, at a small college game in Greensboro, North Carolina, between Emory and Henry and Guilford College. That day there were at best a few hundred people in attendance and maybe a few dozen more listening on AM radio. This night in South Florida, nearly 27 million Americans were watching on television.

From that first game to this last one, there had been two constants. First, my father was on the field. Second, there was one loudmouth guy also in attendance who'd made it his mission in life to remind my father that he was a blind idiot. No, it wasn't the same guy. But it might as well have been. Like some sort of Dickensian Ghost of College Football Games Past, he was there as a proud representative of every man, woman, and child who'd ever shouted at Dad, a lifelong verbal assault stretched out over every game he'd ever worked. This guy screamed from the first row of Dolphin Stadium, convinced that the seven men in stripes had cost his beloved top-ranked Oklahoma team their eighth national title...because, you know, it couldn't have possibly been the

Sooners' suddenly inept offense, gassed defense, two interceptions, or their inability to convert on third down.

No, it was the field judge's fault.

"YOU STUPID ACC REFFFFF!"

Dad never heard him. Just as he never heard anyone at
Guilford in 1972. He was focused on the next play. He was
always focused on the next play. Even as he talked to me in
that moment, his eyes never left the field. He was treating these
final plays the same as he had the other 158 plays of the night,
and the same as he'd handled every play in every single one
of those 403 games before this one. He moved into position,
employing second-nature mechanics that had become muscle
memory, though as the years had ticked by and the game had
sped up, that positioning had been adjusted to cover a much
faster brand of football play and football players. He counted
the Oklahoma defensive players on the field, one to 11. He
awaited the snap. When it happened, he watched his zone,
monitored the players who came into that zone, and managed
it all accordingly.

Both quarterbacks in this game—Tim Tebow and Sam
Bradford—were Heisman Trophy winners, the last two on a
headcount of more than a dozen Heisman winners my father
had shared a field with since 1982, from Bo Jackson and Eddie
George to Gino Torretta and Charlie Ward. A few months
later, eight players in this game would have their names called
in the NFL draft. The following year, another 16 players from
this game would be drafted. In all, more than two dozen players on these two rosters would go on to serve at least a little time on NFL rosters. Both head coaches, Florida's Urban
Meyer and Oklahoma's Bob Stoops, are national title winners
and future College Football Hall of Famers. The first time Dad

shared a field with these two at the same time had been 14 years earlier and on a completely different coast, in San Diego's Holiday Bowl, when Stoops was the defensive coordinator for Kansas State and Meyer was the wide receivers coach at Colorado State.

Florida was grinding along to run out the clock. On a first-down dash that essentially ended the game, quarterback Tim Tebow collided with umpire Tom Laverty, the official perilously positioned behind the defensive line on every play. Tebow—6'3", 250 pounds—crashed into Laverty, a former collegiate offensive lineman who was nearly every bit as big as the quarterback. The impact was a large one, but both men popped up, though Laverty did so with a Tim Tebow cleat mark in his back.

"Ouch!" Dad said, watching the stadium video board for a replay of the pileup, which had happened in the middle of the field, 22 yards away from his post downfield. It might have looked like he was talking to no one in particular, or even muttering to himself. He was known to do that during games. But right now, he was speaking to me. "That's why I like being down here."

He turned his head so that I could see his smiling face from my vantage point on the sideline, standing a few feet behind him. I was covering the game as a senior writer for *ESPN The Magazine*. I'd spent the first three and a half quarters in the cramped auxiliary press box, an unused skybox stuffed with extra stools for writers and their laptops. As per the usual press box rules, media members were allowed to descend to the sideline for only the final few minutes of the game. Usually, I was the last one down there, holding out to watch as much of the game as I could from the better vantage point up top.

But tonight, I'd been the first sportswriter off the elevator, eager to stake out a position as close to my father as my press credentials and stadium security would allow.

Dad had spotted me immediately, and as the plays had moved up and down the field, I had moved with them, just off the shoulder of the field judge, separated only by the thick white painted sideline at our feet. I let him know I was there. "Hey, McGee!"

He turned to face me, but only halfway. He smiled.

"Well," he said, tilting his head toward the scoreboard and referencing a month of pregame predictions of a video game shootout between Tebow and Sam Bradford, "I don't think this one is going to be 52–50, do you?"

I laughed and shouted back. "If they're going to do it, they'd better hurry up!"

The whistle blew. The ball was snapped. Dad launched into action. Another play. A few more seconds off the clock. Then the cycle started over again.

"You get to see your brother?" Dad asked.

"Yep, I went down and saw them at halftime," I replied, pointing to where my younger brother, Sam, and Dad's younger brother, my uncle Danny, were seated in the corner of the lower bowl, right behind where we were now. This was not the first time we had flown to Florida for a postseason game we believed would be Dad's last. But this time, he promised, he was really done. We hadn't been there for his first game in '72; I was a baby and Sam had yet to be born. But there was no way we were missing his last one.

The people sitting around Sam and Danny, as usual, were the families of the other six members of the officiating crew. As the game entered the final minutes, the officials' wives and children and siblings began to breathe easier. There had been no big controversial calls (no matter what the guy in the front row thought) and, more importantly, no one on the crew had gotten hurt. There had been a pause from the families when Laverty went down at midfield, but when he popped back up, they sighed their relief and the game went on.

"Good, I'm glad you got to see them for a minute." Dad nodded as he talked. "That's good."

Whistle. Snap. Play run.

A fellow member of the media, waiting to storm the field as soon the game went final, tapped me on the shoulder and pointed to Dad. My friend wasn't mad, but he was confused. He simply hadn't seen a conversation like this one before. Chatting it up during a live college football game? Between a game official and some guy on the sideline? He knew this was my father and he knew this was my father's final game. All my press box colleagues knew that, because I had a column in the current issue of *ESPN The Magazine* titled A TRIBUTE TO MY FATHER, ACC FIELD JUDGE JERRY McGEE.

"What the hell are you two doing?" he asked.

I reached out, squeezed his arm, and winked. "It's all good, man. We've been having this conversation since I was a kid."

We had. It was a sideline chat that started on November 12, 1983. That was the very first time I'd ever worn sideline credentials, at a contest between the universities of North Carolina and Virginia in Charlottesville, Virginia. I had just turned 13 and was wielding the camera that Santa Claus brought me one year earlier. Sam, three years younger, was there, too. I got run over during the game-winning touchdown run and Sam got into trouble for running onto the field midgame. But we figured out how to keep coming back.

Those in-game chats continued for the next 25 years, as either Sam or I birddogged Dad along sidelines from Duke and West Point to Pittsburgh and Clemson's Death Valley. That's how we learned the game of football, watching from field level as our father made split-second decisions on Saturdays and then walked us through why he did or didn't throw his penalty flag after those decisions were made. We learned the ever-changing college football rulebook in real-time, watching Dad's games in person, watching grainy VHS recordings of those games, listening to him recite those rules aloud as he prepared for exams, and participating in living room walk-though demonstrations/explanations of what we'd just been taught from all of the above. "Okay, this is how the new halo rules will work on punts. Sam, you're the punt returner. Ryan, stand here, you're from the kicking team. Go get your mom. We need a second person for the return team..."

We learned the game of football so much differently than anyone else I knew. The only people I've talked to who seem to understand what I'm talking about when I explain it are the kids of coaches. It's a childhood of Xs and Os, watching fathers spend their summers dissecting game film, knowing that every autumn weekend will never be free for other activities, and that every New Year's holiday will (hopefully) be spent in a hotel and at pre-bowl game events, the reward for all of the hard work put into a (hopefully) successful regular season.

But even those coaches' kids weren't taught what we, the children of officials, were.

What we learned was that there are never two teams on the field when the ball is kicked off. There are three. And that third team, the one in stripes, doesn't arrive in a chartered jet. They ride in coach, sleep in a Holiday Inn Express, take a van to the stadium, and are cussed at along every step of the way. These days, with every game broadcast on television and every play of those games pushed through the prism of social media, the anonymity of their predecessors has long since vanished, and the criticism they receive is no longer limited to the hours surrounding the game itself. Now it never ends. For their efforts, they are handed a check for a few hundred dollars, one they can deposit during the commute to their day jobs on Monday morning.

Yet despite all of that, no one in that stadium each Saturday truly loves the experience more than that third team, the officials. They have to love it. Why else would they do it?

But that third team is not totally alone. They have their families. If you're as fortunate as my brother and I were, then you get to feel like you are on that officiating team. We McGees, we've always been a close-knit family, but the strongest thread of our shared DNA has always been dusted with white sideline paint.

Sam once saved the day on the sidelines at the New Jersey Meadowlands. A chilling autumn downpour prevented Dad and his crew from filling out their penalty cards, the mandatory in-game log of the day's fouls. The instant they would pull the cards from their pockets, they'd become waterlogged. So, Sam filled out their paperwork for them, scribbling blind with a pencil under a poncho. I can guarantee that you he knew the rules better than anyone else on that sideline, including most of the coaches from Duke and Rutgers, or any of the fans hiding under the lip of the upper deck. He was 14.

I once stood on the sidelines at Liberty University and received a question about my in-game chats with the field judge that day, too. "Excuse me, but are officials supposed to be talking with riff-raff during games?" The voice was booming, but pleasant. It was also, thankfully, joking. Reverend Jerry Falwell, the polarizing preacher, political figure, and founder of the school, was smiling in his three-piece suit, the evening news suddenly coming alive right before my eyes. "That's Dr. McGee. He's your father?" Falwell asked. I said yes. "Well then," he said, feigning a reach for his wallet. "Maybe we can work out a deal for a timely pass interference."

Saturday afternoons were also when my brother and I learned how to cuss, listening to people lob colorful adjectives at my father and his crewmates. We spent holidays at bowl games, from Pasadena to San Diego to Memphis to, finally, right here in Miami for the '09 BCS title game. Almost exactly 21 years earlier, on January 1, 1990, we were also together in Miami, just 14 miles to the south at the old Orange Bowl Stadium for another national title game, between Notre Dame and Colorado. There had been four of us there that night, too, but it wasn't Uncle Dan who was with us. It was Hannah McGee, our mother and Dad's wife. Nine years later, she was taken from us unexpectedly. That fall, it was college football that helped heal our hearts. We experienced that together, too.

To us, "Hey, Ref!" was "Hey, Dad." Every new team he saw on the field meant another pennant on the wall of our home basement, covered with the banners of every school he'd officiated, more than 150 of them. Every family dinner out meant another person asking to see Dad's bowl rings or watches, and then us all pausing to see if the person who'd asked ended up making a connection between their favorite team, the games on that jewelry, and Dad. "Wait...you didn't have that pass interference against us in the fourth quarter, did you?!"

So, that's what was ticking away with the clock at Dolphin Stadium on the night of January 8, 2009. Sure, the game was huge. The biggest stage and biggest stakes that the sport had to offer, played by some of the biggest names in college football history. With all due respect to them, for us the moment was even larger than that. The goodbye was imminent. But it wasn't sad. It was a celebration.

As the four zeroes popped up on the clock, the Florida Gators rushed the field to celebrate their national title. The Oklahoma Sooners stood frozen on their sideline, staring at that scoreboard in disbelief. My media colleagues stepped over that sideline onto the field and took off running to the right, headed to the middle of the field to document the championship moment.

Dad ran in the opposite direction, to the left, through the end zone, beneath the goal post, and into the narrow tunnel that led to the officials' locker room. He had always taken great pride in being the first official to get to that locker room postgame, and this time was no different. I had taken off after him and tried to put my arm around him as he left the field, but he was moving so fast that I had to settle for a sprint alongside. He paused briefly, looking up to the left and toward Sam in the stands. Then his cleats left the turf and clacked their way up the concrete tunnel.

As his crewmates arrived, an impromptu receiving line formed, hugs and congratulations, followed by a little business. Dad's final official act in uniform was to read aloud from his penalty card, going through the game's 11 penalties so that the group could check their cards for accuracy before he turned in the official penalty report for review.

When he was finished, the others in the room started the process of showering and packing their ACC travel bags. Laverty pulled off his uniform to show off his Tebow cleat-carved battle scars. Meanwhile, on the tiny TV affixed to the wall of the locker room, Tebow was addressing the media and was asked about the collision. "I felt bad. I had to help him put his shoe back on and everything." The press room erupted in laughter. Laughing at the refs. What else was new? Those being laughed at never heard it. They were too busy packing up.

But Dr. Jerry E. McGee, the man who'd spent his entire adult life sharing football fields with the likes of Donovan McNabb, Ray Lewis, Joe Paterno, Lou Holtz, not to mention Ryan and Sam McGee, went against his instincts and took a seat on a locker room bench. He watched his colleagues as they scurried around preparing for departure. He swigged some Gatorade. He smiled. Everyone else had changed, but Dad was still in his uniform.

"I think I'm just going to wear this home."

TV Timeout
with Tim Tebow

"I ran over a ref in that game?"

It is sometime during fall 2019, outside a football stadium somewhere in the Southeastern Conference. I am talking with Tim Tebow on the bus that serves as the production office of *SEC Nation*, the flagship college football show of ESPN's SEC Network. It has been nearly 11 years since the Gators won the 2009 BCS title and Tebow was named offensive MVP of the game. He is now a TV analyst for the network, and we are coworkers. Until right now, he didn't realize that Dad was one of the officials in his final college game—so until right now, he certainly didn't know that his last college game was also my father's final game.

Like all great athletes, Tebow has an abnormally acute sense of recall. He can tell you in great detail about plays run in certain quarters on certain downs against certain teams from years ago, just as he can recount nearly every pitch he saw while spending his recent summers playing baseball in the New York Mets organization.

But for the life of him, he can't remember running over Tom Laverty in South Florida, the last real play of his legendary college career.

"Was he okay?"

Yes, he was.

"Wait...that wasn't your dad, was it?!"

No, it wasn't.

"Okay, good! Hey, speaking of the refs, do you know what I do remember most about that game? It feels like it's what most people remember about that game other than us winning it, because I still hear about it all the time, even now. I got flagged in that game. It was on that same drive you're talking about, the last one. I had a good run and we got the first down, but I thought that a guy took an extra shot at me in the pile after I was tackled. I was pretty fired up. So, I jumped up and gave the guy the Gator Chomp."

It was Oklahoma's Nick Harris. He didn't really take an extra shot after the play, but he definitely had some something extra to say to Tebow after the first down that essentially clinched the win for the Gators. As Tebow was headed back to his sideline, he reacted by giving Harris a sarcastic "okay, nice tackle" hand gesture...which was indeed followed by quick three-clap version of Florida's signature chomp...which was followed by a yellow flag toss directly at No. 15 and a 15-yard taunting penalty.

"That was not my finest moment," the player with the famously sparkling reputation recalls. "It was the only unsportsmanlike of my career. Like, ever. Youth football, high school, NFL, anywhere."

Tebow pauses, and then repeats himself.

"Wait...that wasn't your dad, was it?!"

No, it wasn't.

"Okay, good!" He repeats, then adds: "Whoever it was, let them know they definitely got that call right."

CHAPTER 1

IF YOU CAN OFFICIATE SIGMA NU VS. THE PIKAS, YOU CAN WORK THE ROSE BOWL

WHEN DISCUSSING HIS FOOTBALL officiating career, one of the most common questions my father receives is the one that goes back to very beginning: How and why in the world does one get started in a line of work that, if all goes as well as it possibly can, one will end up screamed at, scrutinized, and despised by thousands of people on at least a dozen different days each and every autumn?

This was a question that I investigated in depth for an article on ESPN.com in January 2019. An NFL officiating crew failed to flag what looked to be a blatantly obvious and critically important pass interference in the NFC Championship Game between the Los Angeles Rams and the New Orleans Saints. The no-call ended up leading to death threats, caused the crew to move from one hotel to another for the sake of their safety, and ignited a national outrage that extended from the NFL Commissioner's pre–Super Bowl "State of the Sport"

address to the floor of the U.S. Capitol Building, where a Lou-
isiana lawmaker made his case to have the game replayed. I
spent days talking to football officials, college and NFL, active
and retired, with one question in hand: Why in the world
would anyone want to be a football official?!

To a man, and woman, their response was always the same.

Wait, why am I explaining this? Let's let Dad do it, shall we?

Dr. Jerry E. McGee, a.k.a. Dad

They do it because they love it.

I've learned two things about officials over the years. The
first is that they are all human beings. They make mistakes,
just like a player turns the ball over or a coach calls the wrong
play at the wrong time.

The second is that they truly officiate for the love of the
game. They have to, especially now. Youth and high school
officials have to deal with crazy parents, and they are making
no money. Most college officials aren't making much money
either; they all have full-time jobs, and these days their names
are out there on social media.

Never once have I had an official say they are doing it for
the fame or the money. There's not much money and the best
you can do is infamy. They do it because they love it. And
someone else who loved it first introduced them to it.

So, how did my father get started on the four-plus decade
path that ended on the field in South Florida? The answer
to that question has its roots in the very theme of this book.
It was about fathers and sons. Or, in this case, father figures
and sons.

Jerry McGee grew up in the post–World War II Baby Boomer Era in the poor-but-proud textile mill villages that surrounded Rockingham, North Carolina, a town of only a few thousand people at the edge of where Eastern North Carolina starts its transition from the lush green rolling hills of the Piedmont region to the flat, sandy, pine tree-lined Coastal Plain. In those days, every corner of Rockingham was bracketed with massive brick textile mills, the constant clickety-clack from row after row of looms reverberating through the lint-filled air. To most Rockingham kids, the idea of attending college was like scaling Everest or strolling on the moon. But the parental figures of Dad's childhood, blood or otherwise, never once allowed him to believe that a dream and a fantasy are the same thing.

Dad lost his father, Sam McGee, when he was only three months old, taken at the age of 33 by Bright's Disease, a kidney disorder that is treatable now, but not in the 1940s. A few years later, he got a new father when his mother, Mary MacKinnon, met Robert Marshall Caddell. He was fresh home from his service in World War II, Purple Heart in hand after being blown into the Pacific when a Kamikaze plane struck his ship, the USS Daly. Caddell—or as Sam and I would one day christen him, "Pa-Pa"—was a good man and great father. He called little Jerry "Son" and my future father called him "Daddy."

When Dad was 13, Pa-Pa took him up to Durham, North Carolina, to see Duke host Georgia Tech. It was Jerry McGee's first college football game. Pa-Pa always loved the Blue Devils, and the two sat there in the cheap seats at Wallace Wade Stadium, then still Duke Stadium and less than 30 years old, a classic bowl designed to look and feel like the Rose Bowl in

Pasadena. It had in fact hosted the Rose Bowl Game when Dad was an infant and Marshall Caddell was preparing to steam across the Pacific; the game moved to Durham for fear of a Japanese attack on Southern California.

Dad attended Rockingham High School and played on every sports team that school had to offer, but he excelled at baseball. The Rockets played in a classic small-town bandbox wooden ballpark, metal cleats clicking through the cement dugouts while John Phillip Sousa marches played over the loudspeaker during pregame warmups. Young Jerry was skinny but strong, not quite six feet tall with jet black hair and eyes that were always bright despite his Irish squint.

At Rockingham High, Dad met his third father figure, a perpetually smiling coach named Bill Eutsler, who had played at Duke Stadium twice against Wallace Wade's Blue Devils as a Wake Forest Demon Deacon. In Rockingham, like so many blue-collar factory towns across the United States, sports served as both the ultimate escape and also the tool kids used to learn the benefits of hard work and focus. For Dad, the man who guided him through those sports and then throughout most of his adult life was Eutsler, the man he forever called "Coach."

Over the span of 31 years, Coach Eutsler would build Rockingham High School into a classic Southern Friday Night Lights powerhouse, winning 226 games, 13 conference titles, and four state championships. When my father got on Eutsler's radar, the coach was searching for new ways to ensure long-term football success. A big part of that plan was educating the football-playing kids at the junior high schools that fed into Rockingham High on the Bill Eutsler offensive and defensive philosophies. So, he went to those schools, helped them organize football teams, and created his own little Rockingham Rockets football farm system. Every week, playing fields throughout the Sandhills of Richmond County, North Carolina, came to life with the sounds of youngsters running Eutsler's plays in youth football games.

Those games needed referees. So Coach Eutsler recruited some of his most trusted Rocket athletes to grab whistles and do the deed. That included Dad, a former football center and now senior baseball star, known by one and all in Rockingham as "Smoky" McGee. If you visit Rockingham today and mention Dr. Jerry McGee, some folks will know who that is and some won't. But if you drop the name Smoky McGee, the recognition throughout the room is instant.

One day the coach threw Smoky an armload of striped shirts and said, "McGee, you're in charge of the junior high officials." Dad recruited his buddies, two per crew, and sent them off to places that were little more than country crossroads, anywhere in the area with a junior high school that existed in the high school's gravitational pull. They would find an open field, mark off a 120-yard rectangle with a bag of white lime powder, officiate the "game," and receive a couple bucks for their efforts.

After high school, Dad attended college at East Carolina. There was never a discussion of whether he was going to college, only where he would attend. These days the school is East Carolina University, or ECU, with nearly 30,000 students from around the world. Back then, it was East Carolina College, with about 4,000 students, nearly all from the immediate region. Dad, the first member of his family to attend college, was there to learn how to become a physical education teacher and a coach. He was also there to play baseball, making the

Pirates roster as a relief pitcher on a team that made it to the 1963 NAIA College World Series. But he was also paying his own way through school, spending much of his time during each academic quarter trying to figure out how he was going to foot the bill for the next one, $275 at a time.

Dad

At East Carolina I was playing intramural football, and it was so boring. Two-hand touch or flag football. One night during a game I started talking to one of the student officials and I told him I'd worked some games during high school. He said, "Why don't you officiate games with us?" At first, I was like, *I don't know, man, I have a lot going on.* But he told me they'd pay me two bucks a game and I could work three games a night, so six bucks a night and $24 per week. He said, "Beer money." So I did it, and I was pretty good at it.

Coach Jack Boone, the retired ECU football coach who was running the intramural program, soon asked me to help him oversee officiating. I would recruit students to be officials and train them to work football, softball, and basketball games. I did the scheduling and I made sure the facilities were ready to go. I would observe them and do evaluations, and if there was any controversy during a game, I would deal with that, too. I ran it out of my dorm room.

One day during my junior year he asked me to be the student director of intramurals. I told him I couldn't. I had schoolwork, baseball, and was trying to have a social life. Then he told me it included a half-scholarship, $180 a quarter. That sounds like nothing now. But that $180 per quarter changed my life. And I got that through officiating.

While intramural officiating was paying for school, it was also already beginning to school Dad when it came to the backbone principals of officiating games on any level. As he likes to say, "If you can officiate Sigma Nu versus the Pikas, you can work the Rose Bowl."

Think about it. You've got guys out there who are way too emotionally invested in these games. They are trying to impress their girlfriends. They are trying to prove to everyone that they were the best athletes from their high school back home, which included some of the roughest redneck towns in North Carolina. They are playing on a "field" that is essentially a dirt track. They are the same guys with whom, as a student official, you are eating with in the cafeteria and sitting with in class and drinking with on the weekends, so they think as a friend you should always cut them slack during games.

And, oh yeah, some of them are playing half-drunk. Even on their worst nights, the guys on the field in the Fiesta Bowl weren't inebriated. (As far as we know.) Even if they were and someone decided to come after one of the officials during a game, in the Fiesta Bowl, someone else was there to have your back—at least a half-dozen someones. On the intramural field, there was one other official. Maybe.

Speaking of, this feels like as good a time as any for a primer on the makeup of officiating crews. As a kid growing up in an officiating home, knowing the who/what/how of the positions on the field was something I took for granted. But as the years have ticked away, I've been shocked at how many people don't know the roster of every game's third on-field team, and that includes some of my most decorated and respected press box colleagues, men and women who have covered the sport for years. So, here we go...

These days, if you watch a big-time college football game you will see eight officials. Each is assigned to specific positions to watch a specific zone of the playing field, and within those varied zones they usually handle a very different group of players and penalties.

Here's the roster:

–**Referee:** Most people call everyone in a black-and-white striped jersey "ref," but the reality is that there's only one referee. This official is known the "white hat" because they're the only member of the crew wearing one. Positioned in the offensive backfield behind the quarterback, they are looking for illegal blocks, roughing the passer, everything around the quarterback. If you've ever known the name of a football official, it's probably a referee, because they're the one who wears a microphone and explains to stadium and television audiences what's going on after any penalty flag or unusual play. They also get to announce "first down!" after a measurement.

–**Umpire:** Yes, there are umpires in football. Positioned on the defensive side of the line of scrimmage and focused on interior line play, this is the official who is always in the middle of the chaos, dodging linebackers as they chase running backs and running backs as they try to avoid the would-be tacklers. Tom Laverty, the former college lineman who was run over by Tim Tebow, was an umpire. Most umpires are big dudes like Laverty. Now you know why.

–**Linesman, or Head Linesman:** Straddling the line of scrimmage on one sideline, they make sure everyone is where they're supposed to be in relation to that line, watching for offsides, encroachment, illegal men downfield, illegal shifts, and the like. They also watch the sideline when a play comes their way to determine in- or out-of-bounds rulings and are in constant communication with the chain crew to keep them up-to-date on first downs and marking the line of scrimmage.

–**Line Judge:** Straddling the line of scrimmage on the opposite side of the field, their duties are similar to the head linesman, but with the added responsibilities of providing assistance to the umpire on holding calls and the referee on false starts. They're also the keeper of the game clock (yes, that's kept officially on the field, to keep the press box clock operator honest) and responsible for ensuring the quarterback doesn't cross the line of scrimmage before throwing a pass and that the kicking teams don't do the same before the ball is kicked.

–**Field Judge:** They share the same sideline with the line judge, but are positioned further downfield on one side of the defensive backfield, 20 yards or more. They count for 11 defensive players pre-snap and keep the 25-second play clock. This position is best known for handling pass plays or long runs, set up downfield for the express purpose of being in position to handle those plays. Their most common flag is pass interference. This was Dad's position for most of his big college career.

–**Side Judge:** Everything you just read about the field judge applies to this position as well, only the SJ is located on the opposite side of the field, sharing a sideline with the head linesman. Also, all four of these line of scrimmage sentinels also enjoy/endure very direct dealings with the coaches and teams when they want to dispute/discuss the flag just thrown.

–**Back Judge:** This is football officiating's version of a centerfielder, lined up at least 25 yards into the defensive backfield and in the middle of the field. They are responsible for the deep zone and also the game clock. That official you see sprinting alongside a wide receiver who just broke a 40-yard post route and is headed up the middle of the field to the goal line? That's the back judge. And when a kicker sends a ball through the uprights—or doesn't— the back judge and the field judge are the two positioned beneath those uprights to signal whether or not the kick was good.

–**Center Judge:** This is still a new position in college football, introduced in the mid-2010s. They are positioned in the offensive backfield like the referee, but on the opposite side of the quarterback. The official NCAA guidelines that describe the center judge's responsibilities use the word "help" a lot, and they should. That's why the position was created. As the game has increased in speed during this century, that help has been sorely needed, if for no other reason to make sure the ball is spotted correctly and ready to go in the world of no-huddle offenses.

Additional help has been added over the years in the form of an on-site replay official in the press box, an on-site observer/evaluator, officiating "command centers" where the conference coordinator and his team watch every camera from every game, and a national officiating coordinator who is keeping an eye on everything and everyone we just listed, at the 60-plus games being played nationally every weekend.

All the above is an admittedly oversimplified explanation of everyone's duties. But you get the idea. Now imagine subtracting members of that team one at a time and thus taking one, two, three, or even six of each position's responsibilities and dividing them among a much, *much* smaller group.

When Dad finished his college officiating career in 2009, they were using seven-man crews and the command centers were still an experiment. When he started his Division I college career in 1982, those crews had six men. His first small college crews in the 1970s used five officials. In high school football, there were four…and that was only if everyone who was supposed to show up for the game actually did, which wasn't a given.

In 1965, Dad got married, graduated college, returned home to Rockingham, and started a job as an industrial engineer with one of the textile mills, all while serving in the Army National Guard. It was an insanely busy time. Amid it all he received a call from a man named Allen Gaddy.

Dad

Mr. Gaddy was the godfather of high school officiating in the area. He was also regional distributor of Buttercup Ice Cream. He was a little guy, he had kind of big tummy on him, and he was funny. Everyone liked him. He was a good-natured guy. But he didn't take any crap from anyone.

He would officiate high school games on Friday nights and would also do some small college games on Saturdays. When he officiated games, he'd chew tobacco the whole time. He'd be running up and down the field all night with his whistle hanging around his neck and it would bounce up and down on his belly. Then, when the games were done, he'd have brown tobacco juice stains all down the front of his jersey. The first time I saw it, I thought it was blood. I pointed to a big wet red stain right on his gut and he said, "Yeah, some guy kicked me right there earlier." He was lying. It was the tobacco juice coming out of his whistle and splashing all over him when he ran.

Mr. Gaddy would look like a total mess, but there was no one more respected in North Carolina high school sports officiating.

The man some called Daddy Gaddy had heard about young McGee's time on the field at East Carolina and wanted to know if he'd like to drop in on a meeting that he was running with local high school officials. Dad went, and when he walked in the door, he realized that he knew nearly everyone in the room. He'd either played with them or against them as a Rockingham Rocket or, as a kid, had watched them playing for local schools. They were from all the towns in the area, from the northern edge of the South Carolina border up to the southern tip of the fabled golf courses of Southern Pines, North Carolina.

Dad immediately wanted in. Even after Mr. Gaddy informed him that he would have to buy his own uniform and work his first five games without pay. Anyone who wanted to be an official would have to start out losing money. It was the first of a lifelong, neverending list of reasons to not do it, an obstacle course seemingly designed to weed out those who weren't worthy, or perhaps even to prove the insanity of those who were.

It was 1966. Dad worked his first five games and lost his money. Gaddy took young McGee under his wing, as did another veteran Rockingham-based white hat named Jimmy Maske and the regional officiating coordinator, Cecil Longest, who preached advice to Dad that he carried with him until he hung up his last uniform 43 years later: "Stay out the way. Play deep. Only call the obvious stuff. Learn all you can from the guys around you."

The following fall, he worked his first full season of North Carolina high school football, sometimes officiating three or more games in three days, from junior high on Wednesday to junior varsity Thursday to varsity games on Friday nights. The big varsity schools paid $25. The smaller ones paid half that. You could make a little more if you agreed to be the designated driver, though that meant giving up one's late night backseat beer privileges (reminder: this was the 1960s). The guy who lived the furthest away from the destination school would drive, stopping by the homes of the other three members of the crew and picking them up to travel to such exotic locales as Fairmont, Rowland, and Tabor City, to work games on fields that were more sand than grass, instantly filled with puddles of standing water after even the smallest rain shower.

They loved it.

They would sometimes drive hours in both directions to work two-hour games scattered throughout a region of rural North Carolina that covered more than 2,000 square miles, all for the honor of getting dressed in the girls' basketball locker room or in the parking lot next to the car. If it was a local game, they'd dress at home, which always drew interesting looks from other motorists, being passed by a station wagon driven by a man dressed in thick black and white stripes. Those uniforms were self-purchased from the local sporting goods store or Sears & Roebuck. Dad would buy white dress pants and have his new wife and my future Mom, Hannah, sew up the cuffs into the correct shortened, bloomed-out knickers style that he always loathed. His entire career he lobbied to switch to black, track suit-style pants, to no avail. The NCAA did finally introduce them…the year after Dad retired.

During the weekdays, Dad worked. During weeknights, he played semi-pro textile league baseball, while also umpiring church and industrial softball at $8 per game. Every dime went toward Mom's tuition, as she too was now paying her own way through college. On Monday nights, the local Rockingham officials would meet at Mr. Gaddy's office to have a rules discussion, go over the evaluations turned in by the coaches of their last game, receive their assignments for the upcoming week, and eat free ice cream.

In 1967, there were 2,600 officials working high school football games in North Carolina. Dad, in his first full season, received the highest coaches' grade among them. He worked as either a line judge or a head linesman, stationed along the sideline directly in front of the coaches and their teams. But on a four-man high school crew, he was also responsible for however many yards lived between him and the goal line. That's a lot of real estate.

Dad

Working the line of scrimmage in the high school, at the snap you had to know if an offensive lineman moved or if a defensive lineman was offsides. Then you had to watch for holding, which means you couldn't see the guy with the ball coming at you. But if that guy with the ball, the one you can't look for yet, breaks a big play, now you have to take off after him and try to beat him to the goal line, and we had a lot of kids in these games who went on to be college football players.

Man, I was covering 120 freaking yards. It was good to be twenty-something years old.

That's where Dad would end up spending nearly his entire officiating career, on the sideline and downfield, though thankfully, as the years went by and headcounts grew, the amount of space one to had cover was never as ridiculous as in those earliest days.

But what never changed about being in those positions, no matter the level of football, was that the sideline guy is also the guy who delivers the bad news about penalties to the head coach and the guy who has to manage the ire that often comes with that delivery. As a lifelong "people person," Dad was also very good at handling those interactions. His evaluation grades reflected that. But a nice evaluation score certainly didn't mean that 100 percent of the people coaching or working those games were happy 100 percent of the time.

One night at Laurinburg High, the home team scored late and went for the two-point conversion to tie the game. The ball carrier got his foot into the end zone, but the ball never crossed the goal line. Dad signaled no score. Then something whooshed over his head and helicoptered onto the playing field. It was the yard and first down markers, thrown in disgust by the sideline chain crew. They'd decided that they were done for the night. There was still a minute and half left to play.

Dad couldn't help but think he was glad the same hadn't happened during a junior high game in Laurel Hill, North Carolina, a game he'd worked for a friend who was starting a football program where there'd never been one before. When Dad got there, he realized that there were no first down chains

at all. No problem, the friend assured him, producing a pair
of tree saplings connected with 10 yards of rope. If someone
had tried to throw those in protest, it would have been bad.
(By the way, there was also a huge oak tree in one end zone,
but both coaches agreed it wouldn't be a problem because
they'd never complete a pass. Hell, they probably wouldn't
even score.)

Dad

To do this job, you have to learn detachment. Every
game you work is the most important game you've ever
worked, whether it's Michigan at Notre Dame or Rockingham at Hamlet. When I first started working high school
games in Eastern North Carolina, at least a third of the
teams I officiated were being coached by guys I had just
gone to college with. But holding is still holding, no matter
who the people involved are. So I learned very quickly to
check that at the door—relationships, teams you might have
rooted for as a kid, famous names. You can't be objective
if you don't.

In 2002, I worked the Houston Bowl between Southern Miss and Oklahoma State, who had an incredible wide
receiver. I loved watching that kid play. Early in the game
he had a 60-yard catch, but we called it back because I got
him for offensive pass interference. I wasn't alone. Virgil
Valdez, a longtime great official, had it too. Les Miles was
Oklahoma State's coach at the time, and he sent word all
the way across the field to me, "Tell the field judge that's
Rashaun Woods and he's a first team All-American." And
I sent word back to Miles, "You tell Coach that today he's
No. 82."

An official has to remove connections, names, even team brand names, anything that might get in the way of how a game needs to be called. They can be in awe of the experience of walking into Darrell K Royal–Texas Memorial Stadium for the first time, seeing Longhorns mascot Bevo, and hearing the band play "The Eyes of Texas." They can be intrigued by the prospect of watching a Heisman Trophy favorite in person. They can even be excited to see an old friend on a coaching staff.

But once the game clock starts, all that fades into the background. It's two teams led by players and coaches and it's just the next game on the schedule. It's a lesson Dad learned at the very beginning of his career, calling those college intramural and high school games.

Dad

One night we had a big game in Wadesboro, North Carolina, and their head coach was a legend. Ed Emory was an All-American offensive lineman at East Carolina before I was a student there, and he had a North Carolina Sports Hall of Fame coaching career, at several high schools and also at ECU. I was officiating the game with a dear friend of us both, Jerry Brooks, who was from Rockingham and played with Ed at ECU. Both really good, decent, sweet men.

Whenever a crew was done working a game at Wadesboro, they had a standing invitation to stop by this local place called Bowman's Restaurant for a steak and a beer. A table was always waiting in a private room in the back. Ed Emory always made sure of it. This particular night, three of our four guys were East Carolina guys—me, Brooks, and my best friend, Ken

Rankin. Ed loved that. "Alright! Three ECU Pirates, this is gonna be good tonight! We're gonna win tonight!"

In the fourth quarter, this little scatback for Wadesboro breaks an 80-yard touchdown run that is going to win the game. Ken and I are chasing the kid to the goal line, signaling touchdown, and the crowd is going nuts. Then we look back to other end of the field and Jerry Brooks has a flag on the ground. Holding. Now I have to go tell Ed.

"F--king Jerry Brooks called that, didn't he?"

"Yeah, Coach, he did."

"He was my damn college teammate. When your college teammate is doing that to you, you don't stand much of a damn chance, do you?"

Wadesboro loses. We're in the dressing room getting changed and I said to Jerry, "Well, thanks to you there won't be any steaks tonight." But Jerry Brooks insisted we were fine. "I've been friends with Ed Emory since we were 18 years old. He's not that kind of guy. We're going to Bowman's."

We got there and it was like the Long Branch Saloon in Dodge City. We walked in and this old guy was wiping down the bar. He looked up and said, "What the hell are y'all doing here?" The place was full and there had been all of this noise and laughter and people having a good time. But when he said that, it went totally silent.

Jerry says, "Didn't Coach Emory call?" The bartender said, "Hell yeah, he called alright. He said if y'all came in here to have your asses arrested."

That night I think Jerry Brooks learned about detachment.

Another lesson learned early on by any and every sports official is that benefit of the doubt will never be on their side.

Just as it was in the real Long Branch Saloon, those officials' black ballcaps might as well be black cowboy hats, because in the eyes of the audience they are always the bad guys, even when they are going out of their way to do the right thing. That leads to another lesson: no one is ever going to truly look out for them but them.

Dad

We had a game at Massey Hill High School in Fayetteville on a Saturday and it wasn't even our game. We had worked a game on Friday night and Saturday morning the phone rang. It was Mr. Gaddy. He said that they'd had a big mess at Massey Hill and he needed our help. The officials who were supposed to have worked their game the night before had gotten the home and visiting teams mixed up and gone to the wrong stadium, so their game had to be postponed. So, here we come, we're gonna save the day, right?

We came out of the locker room and were walking onto the field and the PA guy comes over the speakers, real sarcastic: "Well, look who showed up tonight. It's those damn officials who couldn't find the stadium last night, but they found it today. Great job, boys. Let's have a hand for the officials." That got the crowd all lathered up—cussing and cat calls and everything.

We stopped at the home bench for pregame, but Mr. Gaddy never even slowed down. He went right up through the stands and climbed the ladder into the press box and for at least five minutes he had his finger in that guy's face. I have no idea what he said to that guy, but when he came back down and we started our pregame, the PA came back over the speakers. This time he was very sincere. "Well, I'd like to apologize to the officials. They worked the game at Lumberton last night and we appreciate them giving us their valuable time tonight. Thank you, gentlemen."

There were always a handful of too-passionate fans. That never changed, from Massey Hill to the BCS Championship Game. But even during nights spent working in some of the darkest corners of the North Carolina countryside, there were only a few times it felt unsafe. The occasional group of over-zealous rednecks would stalk the refs up and down the sideline, threatening to wait for them in the parking lot at night's end. No one ever did, but you'd never know that for sure until you walked out of the locker room later.

One night, Dad went with some friends to watch them officiate a high school basketball game. When they returned to their car to drive home, they found the tires slashed. But that was it. A lot of mean talk, but thankfully none of it was followed up with action. "If I ever thought there was a real chance of trouble, I just stayed as close to Jerry Brooks as I could," says Dad. We McGees aren't big guys. Brooks, the former ECU offensive lineman, was.

Yet another lesson learned in those early years was the importance of timing, in one's life, one's love, one's career, and certainly in one's experiences on the playing field. Dad has earned every bit of success in his life, and there has been a lot. But he is also smart enough to know that there had to be some breaks along the way, timed just right, whether it was a college intramurals director in need of a student's help or a high school officiating coordinator with some open roster spots to fill on Friday nights. And yes, the importance of timing also applies to that coordinator's decision-making during those Friday nights.

Dad

We had a first-round state playoff game at a high school where we had just worked a game a couple of weeks before. In that game, Mr. Gaddy had two or three holding calls against that team. Well, as soon as we walked up, the head coach came running at us, just screaming in Mr. Gaddy's face. "You sonofabitch! How'd you get a playoff game? You screwed us the last time you were here!"

The game started, and the whole first half he just didn't stop screaming at Mr. Gaddy, who was in the middle of the field. Well, I'm a linesman. I'm right there on the sideline with this guy and he is just screaming and cussing over my shoulder the whole first half. I kept warning him, but he wouldn't stop. "I ain't stopping! I hate that sonaofabitch!"

At halftime there was no score. But I was begging Mr. Gaddy, "You have to flag that guy!" He just smiled, tobacco juice running out of his mouth and said, "Don't worry, I'll get him."

Midway through the third quarter, one of the home team players broke a big run for a touchdown. A game-changer. I looked back to the middle of the field and there's Mr. Gaddy standing over his flag. Holding. Home team. The touchdown was coming back.

Now it's my job as the official on the sideline to report the foul to the head coach. I walked over and said, "Coach, do you know what that was?"

He said, "I know exactly what that was. You tell that little sonofabitch I ain't saying nothing else the rest of the night."

That lesson in timing also extended to the larger world outside of football officiating. At the same time Dad was making his way up the North Carolina high school sports ladder, those schools were desegregating. A too-slow process had finally met the requirements of the Supreme Court's 1954 *Brown v. Board of Education* ruling by the 1971–72 school year. That meant a merging of officials as well, with split crews of men of different skin tones who used to work their Friday night games separately. That transition certainly didn't go smoothly everywhere, but for Dad and his crew black and white went together as naturally as the stripes on their shirts, even as they traveled the backroads of North Carolina. There were certainly some, "Y'all really got those guys with you?" reactions from coaches, fans, and restauranteurs as the integrated crews walked onto their fields and into their burger joints, but they amounted to little more than side-eyed looks and under-the-breath comments.

The only exception was a roadhouse in Ellerbe, North Carolina, a popular spot for Dad and the other Rockingham-based officials to stop for a beer on the way home. The place had only one long bar, but the patrons' side of that bar was divided by a wall, marked "Whites Only" on one side and "Coloreds Only" on the other, with the bartender moving back and forth between the two ends. Dad's new officiating crew, the one that blurred the lines that built that wall, decided to stop and walk into the whites-only side together.

They were escorted out.

Unbeknownst to Dad, his future college officiating teammates were enduring similar experiences as they worked their ways up ladders in other southern states. That included men of color, such as Virgil Valdez, the man who'd joined forces with Dad to make that Houston Bowl pass interference call that angered Les Miles. Valdez, who attended segregated schools in Miami, went on to work more than a dozen postseason games, including two Rose Bowls, and the two most legendary "Wide Right" contests between Miami and Florida State.

Dad

I thought about that night in Ellerbe at my final college football game. The white hat in that game was Ron Cherry. He was the first black referee to work a national championship game. It should have never taken that long. But I was so very proud to be in that game with him.

Dad received another glimpse into his future in 1969. A grainy, black-and-white, barely viewable glimpse into his future. It was a game in Whiteville, North Carolina, the last decent-sized town that most people see as they drive across the southeastern corner of the state en route to the beach. WILM-TV in Wilmington had chosen the contest to be its High School Game of the Week. The local station would tape games on Friday night using no more than a couple of clunky video cameras, to be replayed on Saturday morning. The officiating crew was impossibly excited. The crowd was fired up. All hands were in the air as the teams were set for kickoff. Then Dad blew his whistle. The four-man crew met in the middle of the field and Gaddy said, "McGee, what the hell are you doing?"

Dad whispered into the ear of Joe Gwinn, head linesman and insurance salesman. Gwinn calmly walked over, picked up the football, and moved it five yards. In their excitement, they had marked the ball at the 35-yard line instead of the 40. It was a nice save.

Early the next morning, after only a few hours' sleep, Dad and Mom woke up in their newlywed apartment, located behind a countryside mansion that had once belonged to my mother's family, now owned by a distant cousin. That house had the biggest TV to be found in the rural outskirts of Rockingham and a big enough TV antenna on the roof to snatch up a little bit of signal from Wilmington, 150 miles away. So that's where Dad was headed.

The picture was bad at best, but it was there. Amid the snow and the grain, he could see himself, trucking it up and down the football field with the ease of a twentysomething kid.

It was his first televised game. There would be so many more. But not quite yet.

Coach's Timeout
with Ed Emory

"Bowman's. That place was good. But they didn't put up with any riffraff."

Ed Emory, 75, is laughing about the night he had his officiating friends thrown out of Wadesboro, North Carolina's finest restaurant. It is a beautiful autumn Saturday at Wingate University during the 2012 college football season and we are chatting in the president's box at Irwin Belk Stadium. We have both been invited into that box by the president of the university, Dr. Jerry E. McGee, but Dad has headed downstairs for some sort of official halftime presidential duties. During his dual-life as a college official and college administrator, the only fall weekends he spent off the playing field were homecomings at the schools of his employment. Yes, sometimes the day job won out. With Dad downstairs, Coach Emory is chatting me up.

In the years following the Bowman's ejection, Emory constructed an incredible coaching résumé that took him through several ACC schools before he became a head coach at East Carolina. He led his alma mater to one of its most memorable seasons, an 8–3 campaign in 1984 that ended with an AP Top 20 ranking. The Pirates' only losses that year were to Florida, Florida State, and Miami.

Emory grew up with a severe speech impediment, but overcame that to become an All-American lineman at ECU and an all-world talker as a coach. In 1966, he made national news when *Sports Illustrated* reported on Emory taking a stance against the Ku Klux Klan in Wadesboro when his efforts to integrate the high school football team were met with resistance. Among the first African American kids Emory welcomed onto his team and then defended from the bigots was Sylvester Ritter, who went on to become a professional wrestling superstar known as the Junkyard Dog.

I first got to know Emory through my very first sportswriting gig, covering high school football for the Monroe (North Carolina) *Enquirer-Journal*. I was in Wadesboro a lot. He wasn't coaching then, but he was always around. He returned to the sidelines a few years later, leading Richmond County High School, what used to be Dad's Rockingham High. In six seasons, he went 77–7.

As we watch Dad hand out plaques to Wingate athletes on the field, Coach Emory is in full talking mode. "All those years your daddy made that drive from Rockingham to Wadesboro to referee my games, and then when I was at Richmond County years later, I was making the same drive in reverse. I lived in Wadesboro and drove over to Rockingham to coach.

"Yeah, that one time we ran him out of town because our team lost. He's never let me forget it. But, you know, if I lost a game, they would run me out of town, too. Problem was, I had to come back there to work on Monday, whether they were mad at me or not."

I ask Ed Emory if he was ever refused service at any restaurant because the hometown fans were too angry to let him eat there.

"One time. And you know what? I think it was in Rockingham. I always wondered if maybe your daddy and Jerry Brooks were finally getting their revenge."

CHAPTER TWO

BIG TIME,
SMALL COLLEGES

WHEN ALLEN GADDY wasn't selling ice cream, munching on chaw, officiating high school games, or shouting down public address announcers, he was spending his Saturdays calling small college football games. In the Carolinas, there have always been plenty of those games to work. Seemingly every town of any size also houses a college campus. Daddy Gaddy worked in the Carolinas Conference, a collection of then-NAIA schools located primarily in North Carolina that included Elon College in Burlington, Guilford College in Greensboro, and Catawba College in Salisbury.

No one from the Carolinas Conference ever officially invited Dad to attend any of their officiating meetings or clinics—certainly not the coordinator, Mr. Joby Hawn, the former ACC coordinator who now oversaw the small schools of the region. But Dad showed up anyway. In 1971, Mr. Gaddy had simply said, "Jerry, I'm going to a college officiating clinic this weekend at Wake Forest, and I want you to go."

Officiating clinics are the big offseason meetings held by each conference, weekend-long affairs designed to run officials through a ringer of physical exams, rules tests, film study, and a dreaded timed mile run. Those clinics are also the only time of year when every official from their respective conference is in the same room at the same time, as opposed to being scattered across the college football map every autumn weekend. So while the clinics are always hard work, they are also always a good time, discussions of rules changes and new on-field mechanics punctuated with war stories about crazy calls and crazier coaches.

Dad sat with Mr. Gaddy at the Carolinas Conference clinic and tied to soak up everything he possibly could. He knew—or at least knew of—a lot of the guys in the room, almost all of them having moved up from the North Carolina high school ranks. The following year, he received an official invitation to attend the clinic. That next fall, he was assigned two college football games as a line judge.

Just as Mr. Gaddy had hoped, showing up uninvited had paid off for his protégé.

On September 16, 1972, Jerry McGee stepped onto the field at Guilford College's Armfield Athletic Center as America's newest college football official. The home team Quakers were hosting the Emory & Henry Wasps. He was fully focused on the task at hand, but he was also fully aware of what was at stake. Over the years, he had friends from his Rockingham high school crews who'd gotten the call up for a college tryout...and it hadn't gone well. At all. One pal got so worked up that he called 13 holding penalties. In one game. The other, a big-bodied lineman-turned-umpire/middle-of-the-field official was sent out of his natural position to back judge, way downfield from the line of scrimmage, to enforce a list of rules he'd never had to worry about before. A lifetime of watching for holding and offsides does not translate into properly policing pass interference.

Their collegiate careers each lasted one game.

Dad

I was a nervous wreck. I had worked a huge high school game on Friday night and got home at midnight. I was driving from home to Greensboro at 6:00 AM and I bet I didn't sleep at all. I just didn't want to mess anything up. Like, I didn't want to leave something I needed at home, or be late, or make any stupid mistake like that. We had our pregame meeting at a room in the Coliseum Motel. I was so jumpy. Then we went over to the stadium, right around the corner.

I think there were 300 people in the stadium. Maybe. The night before at my high school game, we'd had 4,000 people.

Right before the game, I was talking with the back judge and he was a little bitty guy, but everyone knew he was a good downfield official. He could run like a deer. He had these thick glasses and he said to me just before we took the field, "Jerry, you need to ask me anything before I take my glasses off?"

He had hearing aids and they were built into the frame of these glasses with lenses that looked like the bottom of a Coca-Cola bottle. So, he pulled them out, took the glasses off, stuck it all into his pocket, and ran off.

The umpire walked over to me and said, "Well, Jerry, when you dreamed of officiating your first college football game, did you think it would be with a blind, deaf dwarf?"

I wasn't so nervous after that.

Once the game started, it took a few minutes, but when my pregame butterflies were gone, I settled into my routine and it felt like just another game. But as the game went on, I thought about how much easier it was. There was room to work. The field was flat. There was grass—like, really nice grass—and the yard lines were well-marked. The play was so much cleaner. There weren't a lot of sloppy, dumb, high school mistakes being made. And I could actually see! It was a day game. Every high school game was on Friday night under bad lights.

It felt special. I really loved it. My check was $40.

By 1975, Dad had been assigned a 10-game schedule, his first full collegiate season. By then the coordinator was a legendary official, Wilburn Clary. The man they called "W.C." oversaw the officiating for the small colleges of the Carolinas and was himself still on the field, as he had been since 1939. He worked 375 college games in all, including Peach, Orange, and Sugar Bowls, spending most of his career in the Atlantic Coast Conference, the league of Clemson, Georgia Tech, and the teams of Tobacco Road. In 1989, Clary became only the sixth official to be recognized by the College Football Hall of Fame. He was no-nonsense. He demanded excellence. But he also loved his work.

Now he was Dad's newest officiating mentor.

Dad

Mr. Clary always said to us before a game, "Anybody in the stands could referee 95 percent of the plays that are going to happen here today. You're here to officiate the other five percent. There is going to be a long play, a fumble, someone's going to kick it out of bounds, something goofy is going to happen in this game. There aren't many people who are willing to try and handle that. That's why you are here today."

The NAIA, the National Association of Intercollegiate Athletics, was birthed directly from the mind of Dr. James Naismith, inventor of basketball. He sought an organization to handle the governance of his newest brainchild, a national collegiate basketball tournament. Eventually, the NCAA became the governing body of big-time college sports and the NAIA settled into its role as the happy home for America's small colleges, a proud confederation of mostly church-tied liberal arts schools. At the start of 2020, there were 251 NAIA schools. In 1975, as Dad embarked on his first full season as a college football official, that membership was 56. The Carolinas and their bordering states were packed with NAIA powerhouses, including Elon, Wofford, Presbyterian College, and Carson–Newman.

There were small college All-Americans all over every field, from Carson–Newman's Tank Black (before he became a notoriously successfully sports agent-turned-convicted felon) to Elon's Bobby Hedrick, who led the Fighting Christians to the 1980 national title by way of 5,605 career rushing yards. At the time, it was the second-highest rushing total of any running back on any level of college football, trailing only Heisman Trophy–winner Tony Dorsett.

From little stadiums tucked into the autumn-painted Blue Ridge Mountains to the pottery kiln–hot playing fields of the Carolina Sandhills and along the Atlantic coast, the football was good. But the characters were better.

In the final game of one of Dad's first small college seasons, two bad teams were playing out the string, eager to get disappointing seasons over with. To makes matters worse, it was a cold, drizzly, muddy day. The home team busted off a nice long run, but it was called back. Offensive holding. The next series they completed a 20-yard pass. It also came back;

offensive holding again. A few minutes later, another nice play, another penalty. Yes, another offensive holding call.

An incredulous member of the penalized team approached the officials. "Goddammit! Who keeps holding?!" They told him it was No. 75. He turned to his team, hands on his hips. "Goddammit, 75, quit holding! Where is 75? Who be 75?!"

"Hey, man," one of his teammates replied, pointing at his jersey, "You be 75."

"Damn. I do be 75."

Dad

I'd had the same team three times in one season. That never happened in small college ball, but it did this year. A big part of my job my entire career was to get the captains from the locker room for the pregame coin toss.

So I go to get the captains from this team I'd seen three times in the same fall, and this one guy, he's just huge. He looks at me, looks over at his teammates, and then back at me. Finally, he walks over to me and he says, "Hey man, every time I see you, there you are."

I knew what he meant. We'd seen each other three times in, like, two months. The back judge, a guy I'd never worked with before, heard what the kid said and he replied, "Yeah, and of all the people he knows, you're one of them."

Jokes aside, Dad knew a lot of people. Still does and always has. He's always had the gift of making people he's just met feel like they are old friends and making all his old friends feel like they are his best friend. Much as it had been on the high school sidelines, he found that the small college coaching staffs were full of former East Carolina classmates and coaches.

That made for an exciting but awkward exchange back at Guilford College in '73. The Quakers had lost 33 games in a row. But with a two-touchdown lead in the fourth quarter over Randolph–Macon, that streak would finally end. The Guilford coach was Dr. Henry VanSant, a former East Carolina football player, assistant coach, and close personal friend of line judge Jerry McGee. A little too close.

Dad

There was still a good bit of time left in the game, and all of a sudden someone started hugging me, right there on the sideline. It was Henry. "Jerry! We're going to win the game! We're going to win the game!"

I said, "Dammit, Henry, the game is still going on! People can't be seeing you hugging on me!" and I pushed him away.

The game ended and Guilford won for the first time in, like, four years. Everyone on the team ran out on the field and they were hugging each other. But Henry came running back to me and started hugging me again. "We won, Jerry! We won!" He begged me to stay and have dinner with him to celebrate. I told him I had to get on home, but he kept insisting. His wife was out of town, and he didn't want to eat alone. That was the only game he won that year. They went 1–9. It was the only year he coached the team at Guilford. He said to me, "Oh, hell, stay around. I have to celebrate with someone, and you might be my only friend on campus today."

So, I stayed, and he took me to dinner at the on-campus cafeteria. There's the football coach and me, eating together in the cafeteria after the big win.

But here, at the next level of officiating, Dad wasn't only reconnecting with old friends. He was also making a lot of new ones, some of whom he would share locker rooms and playing fields with for the next several decades. Many of the officials he worked with in the Carolinas Conference and its successor, the South Atlantic Conference, were the same teammates he would go on to be crewed with at places like Notre Dame and the Rose Bowl.

As great as the funny stories are, they were merely punctuation to the real story of working small college games, the round-the-clock and round-the-calendar hard work that went into improving one's craft. When Dad and his weekend coworkers were together, they had constant conversations about mechanics, how to best position themselves to keep watch over their designated zones of the field but also to provide backup for their crewmates.

Dad

My philosophy was always, okay, my judgment is pretty good; what I need to work on is positioning. Where I struggled making calls was whenever I was out of position. If I could make sure that I was in the right position, then I could get the call right.

I have told young officials all the time, "We are all human beings and we are all making judgment calls." Sometimes we're going to be wrong. But you can always be 100 percent right mechanically. You can 100 percent be in the right place. You can't control what's happening with the football or in a game. But you can control mechanics.

An official's playbook is no different than it is for a player. If you are in the right place at the right time, you have a chance to get it right. If you aren't, you don't. And that extends to the other officials on your crew, too. If you know that guy is going to be where he is supposed to be, then you don't worry about him. Just like Joe Burrow, the former LSU quarterback, knew he didn't have to worry about those wide receivers being where they were supposed to be when they were supposed to be there. If they run the playbook the way it is drawn up, then he can worry about making the throw, not about whether his guy is going to be there. If I am a field judge and I know the back judge is good on his mechanics, then I can worry about my zone and my guys right in front of me, and not worry about what's going to happen if they get past me and some guy is back there in the wrong place and in position to screw up.

Those early days, with no film and no games on TV, that meant a lot of talking about mechanics. That's all we had.

The responsibilities of an official aren't limited to only those times when the game clock is running. There are also pregame duties. As he's already explained, Dad was always responsible for retrieving the captains from the locker room for the pregame coin toss. And when the game started, the seconds leading into every play meant counting the number of players on the field on defense and the seconds after every play meant changing out footballs with the sideline ball boys and delivering the new ball to the line of scrimmage. And between all of that, *oh yeah*, was watching the play, following the positioning and mechanics determined by the conference coordinator as the best manner to watch that play. If there was a flag on the play, no matter whether Dad threw it or not, as one of the officials who spent his entire day on the sideline, he was also the messenger whom the coaches often wanted to shoot.

The officials who took all those responsibilities seriously would no doubt get a look from the next level, offered a chance to work games at places like Clemson's Death Valley or perhaps even a postseason bowl game in Atlanta, Memphis, or Miami, legendary stadiums where the footballs were new, the showers worked, and someone would actually pay to have you stay in a hotel room.

But for now, their Saturday routines weren't much different than they had been while working high school games. The pay certainly wasn't much better, starting out at $40 per game versus $25. But the football was. Dad realized quickly that he was having to adjust his reaction time—not to mention the head start he gave himself when covering deep pass plays—to the speed of small college players versus those from the public high schools, even with the increase from four- to five-man crews. The playbooks being utilized were a little more complicated, though only a little. But many of the locker rooms were still so small that only two guys could get dressed at once—if there was a locker room at all. Some schools would book a room at a local motel so that the crew could meet, change, and drive over in uniform.

Dad

At Carson–Newman they would always have a room for us at this little motel, doors that opened to the parking lot, like you saw a lot back then. I had driven all the way up from North Carolina into Tennessee with an official named Bill Wampler, a guy I ended up working games with for a couple of decades. We got there and the clerk tried to act like he didn't know we were supposed to have a room. Obviously, he'd sold it. So, he called the manager and that guy let him have it. He hung up and grabbed his keys and said to follow him.

We walked all the way to end of the building and he unlocked all of these locks on the door and said, "Y'all can change in here." When he opened the door, feathers flew out all over the place. They were using this old hotel room as a storage room, and I guess it had been full of old mattresses and pillows. Damn feathers were everywhere. And we're trying to change into our uniforms. We were covered in feathers.

Some of the other guys got there later and when they walked in Wampler said, "We've got some eggs over there in the corner and we're going to need you guys to take turns sitting on those for a while."

Twelve years later, Bill Wampler and I were officiating together in the Orange Bowl. The accommodations were a little nicer.

Like that day in Jefferson City, Tennessee, there were plenty of times when everyone opted out of the postgame shower. If not for feathers, then because the bathroom tiles were covered in a half-inch of mildew. That made for some rank-smelling car rides. And now those car rides, to faraway colleges instead of regional high schools, were much longer than they used to be. On occasion, they were much longer than originally planned.

Chowan College, now Chowan University, is located in Murfreesboro, North Carolina, a town tucked into the northeast corner of a state that is notoriously wide. Chowan is almost in Virginia and almost in the Outer Banks, but not really close to anywhere. In the 1970s, the Chowan Braves were a junior college, coached by small college legend Jim Garrison, winner of 182 games and inducted into so many sports halls of fame that Chowan named its own hall of fame after him.

Dad's first interaction with Garrison was during a pregame walk of the field at what is now known as Garrison Stadium. It is customary for officials to take a stroll around the field long before kickoff to ensure there are no unforeseen safety issues. At the highest levels, that meant checking to see that the Astroturf at Veterans Stadium in Philadelphia wasn't bunched up in the middle of the field (which it had a tendency to do). At the small college level, that might mean telling the grounds crew guy that he can't leave his lawnmower parked at the 25-yard line.

This particular day, Dad noticed that an oak tree outside the stadium had grown to the point that it was hanging over the back of the end zone. He pointed it out to Garrison, who assured the officials that he'd been at Chowan 30 years and no one had ever hit that tree. Dad informed him that the ground rules would be as follows: if a Chowan player threw a pass that hit the tree, it would be ruled incomplete. But if a visiting player hit the tree it would be ruled a touchdown. The next time the crew returned to Chowan, the tree was gone.

Garrison was known for winning, but was also renowned for his keen eye when it came to evaluating young officiating talent. Every official at every level of every sport is under constant surveillance and scrutiny, and those evaluations are ultimately the determining factor in where that official is allowed to work and where he or she will never be allowed to work, be it leagues, levels of leagues, or the postseason games that come with them. And no, this is isn't about the opinions of fans or TV analysts. It's about postgame job evaluations filled out by conference supervisors, conference at-game observers, fellow members of each crew, and, yes, the head coaches of each team in each game. And while most coaches don't have time to fill out the paperwork that comes with Heisman ballots, All-Conference selections or even the Top 25 Coaches Poll, they never skimp on their duties when it comes to sending their opinions on an officials' performance to the conference office on Sunday mornings.

Dad

Yeah, some of the guys took that job a little too seri-ously. At the small college level, you would actually hand the coach your evaluation card prior to the game. We had a guy at Catawba College who got all worked up during a game and started running up and down the sideline, holding that evaluation card in his hand, pointing it at us and screaming. "You just wait until I turn this in, you S.O.B.! You're going back to high school!"

At Chowan, Garrison always provided unemotional, smart, detailed feedback on every official he saw in action. He was in constant communication with W.C. Clary and their mutual friend, Norval Neve (pronounced "Nave"), the officiating coor-dinator for the ACC. Neve was cut from the same old-school granite as Clary, but employed a drill sergeant–like approach to the job that sometimes managed to even make Mr. Clary look slack.

Together, Clary and Neve (Dad called them Mr. Clary and
Mr. Neve, just as he had done with Mr. Gaddy) had a pretty
nice little farm system of their own working, earmarking good
young talent for potential promotions into the collegiate big
leagues and Garrison's evaluations were a key component of
their process. So, to get their guys in front of Garrison's eyes,
they made sure that all of their officials made at least a trip or
two each season to Chowan, no matter how long that trip
took.

Dad

We all knew that if Coach Garrison gave a good review
to Mr. Neve, then that probably meant that you were going
to get a real look from the ACC and you might be on your
way to bigger games. So, you never complained about going
to Chowan, but man, it was hard to get to.

There was a group of really good officials based out of
Greenville, South Carolina. Clark Gaston, who had played
offensive line at Clemson under Frank Howard, and Joe
Long, Rod Dailey, Gil Rushton—these are all guys I went
on to work with in the ACC for years. They had to make
the drive from Greenville to Chowan. That takes seven or
eight hours. It's a night game, so they leave out at dawn and
head east.

They're riding along, all in one car, and start scrolling
through the AM radio to try and find some games to listen
to. As they go along, different games are tuning in and out.
Finally, somewhere around Raleigh, five hours from home but
still two hours from Chowan, they get a good signal and they
hear the play-by-play guy:

"Now it's third-and-six for the Braves...the Braves get a great stop on that play...the Braves have it deep in their own territory..." Well, these guys in the car, they've been driving through North Carolina listening to the Demon Deacons and the Tar Heels and the Wolfpack and now they're asking, "Who the hell are the Braves?" Then the play-by-play guy is taking it to a commercial break and he says, *"At the end the third quarter, Chowan leads 21-7..."*

For some reason, the game had been moved from night to day, and without cell phones or the internet, these guys never got word. So, they stopped in Raleigh, got something to eat, and headed back home. I'm sure they were also wondering who the hell had shown up to work their game.

Rod Dailey said, "Well, I really enjoyed spending the day with my friends, but 10 hours was a little too far to drive for a bad barbecue sandwich."

With all those officials from everywhere on the map driving across all over to get to wherever, having all five members of a crew get where they were supposed to be and when could be a bit of a challenge, especially when those officials were still trying to double-dip with Friday night high school games and Saturday small college contests.

For a contest between Samford and Guilford, there would be a split crew, meaning that some members of the five-man officiating team would be from one conference and others from another. That used to be standard operating procedure for cross-conference games and remained so all the way through the 1980s. Dad and two colleagues from the Carolinas Conference would be joined by a pair of officials from Alabama, home state of the Samford Bulldogs.

At 10:00 AM, three hours before the 1:00 PM kickoff, it was time for the officials' pregame meeting. The guys from Alabama weren't there. At 11:30, still no sign. The white hat looked at his two crewmates and said, "These sumbitches aren't coming!" They decided to go back to their JV high school mechanics. The referee would work the middle of the field; Dad, as line judge, would work the line of scrimmage; and the third guy, the back judge, would cover the entire defensive side of the field.

Fifteen minutes before kickoff, Dad heard someone screaming "Hey, ref! HEY, REF!" but ignored it like he always did. Finally, with kickoff looming, he turned around and looked. There were two guys in black and white stripes standing outside the gate. It was the Alabama boys. They'd worked a high school game in their home state the night before and were running late, way late, and they'd tried to talk their way into the stadium by explaining to the security guard, "We're the damn referees!" The office at the gate replied, "Looks to me like the damn referees are already on the field."

They ran in, with minutes to spare, and received their assignments from the white hat, umpire, and back judge. They didn't like them. "But I'm a referee and he's a head linesman!" the late arrivals informed their new teammates.

"No, we already had our meeting, and you weren't there," the incensed white hat replied. "You mother----ers are what I say you are."

The game went fine and the Alabama boys left for home, making a 1,000-mile round trip to spend no more than perhaps four hours at Guilford College. But, hey, they made $60 apiece.

Dad

We had a game at Lenoir–Rhyne one afternoon, and the referee and the umpire went to meet with the head coaches prior to the game, which is their standard operating procedure. But they came back way too soon and said that the head coach needed to see me. It was my friend, Dr. Henry VanSant, the one I'd had to fight off the hugs from at Guilford. He was now the head coach at Lenoir–Rhyne, and he had a problem.

I go down there and he says to me, "Jerry, the visiting team has shown up with their home uniforms, their dark uniforms. The rules say that visitors are supposed to wear white." We went down to see the visiting coach, and he said, "We're going to wear these uniforms, this is what we're wearing." When Lenoir–Rhyne offered up their white practice jerseys, the other coach said, "We came to play, not to practice." Eventually, we convinced him to do it. It was either they did it, or they had to go back home and get their white jerseys, or we don't play the game.

A few minutes before the game, the home coach comes to me again. Another problem: the visitors had forgotten to bring their headsets for the sideline coaches to communicate with the coaches in the press box. The rules state that if one team doesn't have them, no one gets to have them. So, Lenoir–Rhyne agreed to share some of theirs with the visiting team. Problem solved, again. Let's play ball.

The whole game, the visiting coach was just screaming at us. "I can't wait to report on you guys! We haven't gotten a close call yet!" Just nonstop.

With about 20 seconds left in the game, Lenoir–Rhyne is up by three and they have to punt it away. Now the visitors have the ball with eight seconds to play, a chance to win the game. But they ran the ball off tackle, the clock runs out, and

the game ends. We start running off the field and here comes
the coach, just losing his mind. "Where the hell are you going?"
"Coach, we're going home."
"But you can't go home! That was just the end of the third
quarter!"
The next week he was fired for coaching while inebriated.
Small college football, man.

The occasional drunk notwithstanding, Dad's experience
with the coaches of small college football was a great one,
especially when he reached out for feedback on how to do
his job better. At this same time, he had started working on a
small college campus himself, as a fledgling administrator at
Gardner–Webb College, located in Boiling Springs, North Carolina, squarely in the middle of the South Atlantic Conference.
The Running Bulldogs were also a member of that conference.
That meant that Dad couldn't work Gardner–Webb games, his
first foray into officiating's conflict of interest rules which state
an official can't be assigned to games involving their alma mater,
their children's alma maters, a school located in their city of
residence or, as in this case, a school where they are employed.

There was, however, a big advantage to working at a school
whose team played the teams he officiated on Saturdays. It was
Dad's introduction to film study. In the late 1970s, only a tiny
number of college football games were televised—and certainly
not any small college contests. But teams, even small college
teams, were regularly shooting film of their games and exchang-
ing that film with their opponents. It wasn't great. In the words
of Dad, most of the Super 8mm footage was so fuzzy it was
hard to tell a football from a pair of cleats or a pair of cleats
from a helmet. But it was still a way to watch himself and other

officials to take note of positioning, mechanics, and, clarity willing, whether a foul called had been worthy of the flag thrown.

He went to the Gardner–Webb coaching staff with a request. It was a group of real pros, led by head coaches Oval Jaynes, who would go on to be a high-powered administrator at Auburn, Colorado State, and Pittsburgh, and Tom Moore, who came to GWC to replace the departed Jaynes after a decade on the staff at Clemson. Dad gave them his schedule and asked them to let him know if the film of any of his games made it into their office. They did. And that led to many nights of Dad sitting alone in the empty football coach's office, watching himself on a little pull-down movie screen, fine-tuning his on-field mechanics.

Dad

What a huge advantage that was, to have that perspective of the importance of positioning, being in the right place at the right time to make the right call. And it wasn't just about watching me, it was about watching everyone on the field. It was about how we all worked together and if one guy wasn't doing what he was supposed to, how much that hurt the rest of us.

Before that, I would watch any football I could, just to see how games were officiated. But back then, in the '70s, there was only one college game on TV per weekend, two at most, and I was usually working a game myself and couldn't watch it. There were no VCRs back then. I would try to get back home and watch big college games on Saturday nights and NFL games on Sunday and Monday night to see how they did it, and even though there were a lot of differences in how the NFL and college handled mechanics, what struck you was how precise they were. Those guys were never caught out of position. In the

NFL they always operated from a place of calmness. In college there was a lot of nervous energy on the field and guys were running all over the place. The NFL guys were never rattled, never got excited, always treated every game and play the same. I loved watching Gerry Austin, who was in the ACC and then went on to the NFL and worked several Super Bowls.

I would also have talks with the coaches at Gardner–Webb, like Oval and Tom, about how they liked to interact with officials, and how much different it was at the next level of the college game. They also talked to me about coaching tendencies, why they did certain things at certain times. Coaches scout teams for tendencies and strengths and weaknesses, how their opponent will react in certain situations or how a coach will act in certain situations, and I learned how to do that, too. Every good official needs to know those things about the teams they are going to be on the field with before they get there. That's a big part of being prepared.

Most of time at the small college or high school level, that's all eyeballing on the field or asking other guys for information. Being able to see it on film and have a discussion about it with smart coaches, what an advantage that was as I was still learning about the job. I felt like I was improving pretty quickly.

Still, the timeline for any official, no matter what advantages they might find to accelerate their development, is an exercise in forced patience. By the end of the 1980 season, Dad had worked 80 small college games over eight seasons, the last six full-time. But at the end of that season, a letter had arrived at the house. It was from Greensboro, North Carolina, and the envelope was embossed with the logo of the Atlantic Coast Conference.

Some big decisions were about to made. And Jerry McGee wasn't going to make them alone.

Coach's Timeout
with Oval Jaynes

"Everybody thinks that the coaches and referees are supposed to hate each other all the time, but in reality, most of us are pretty good friends."

It is Thanksgiving week 2018 and I have Oval Jaynes on the phone. He is somewhere in the North Carolina mountains and I am somewhere in the middle of Texas and we are trying to shout our way through spotty cell service. I have known Coach Jaynes since I was in elementary school, when he was head coach at Gardner–Webb and was letting Dad set up in the offices of the Running Bulldogs to watch game film.

He left Gardner–Webb in 1978 to be an assistant coach at Wyoming. Then he was associate athletic director at Auburn in the early 1980s, also known as the Bo Jackson Era, and went on to serve as AD at Colorado State, Pittsburgh, Idaho, Chattanooga, and Jacksonville State. I have called him for a story I am writing for ESPN.com on Jackson, specifically the play that won Jackson the '85 Heisman Trophy, when he sailed over the goal line to defeat Alabama in the Iron Bowl, also known as "Bo Over the Top."

But Jaynes has done what so many in college football do whenever I call them for quotes. He has steered the conversation away from my intended topic with one question: "How's your Dad doing?"

Jaynes is a North Carolina native and only a few years older than Dad, so their connection runs much deeper even than Gardner–Webb. They don't share a handful of friends. All their friends are mutual friends. He retells the story of Dad watching film in his office at Gardner–Webb. "If my players had been as serious as your daddy was about watching game film, I would have won more games."

But then he recounts a story I had heard from Dad, but always thought might've been a little too good to be true.

"I was in my final football season as athletic director at Pittsburgh and Johnny Majors was in his last year as our head football coach. That would have been 1995." Jaynes had hired Majors three years earlier after the coach had been ousted from his alma mater, Tennessee. It was an ugly affair. I know because I was a member of the student film crew at Tennessee and had grown close to Majors, spending nearly every fall football practice for three seasons on his tower as he watched over his offense and shouted "CHECK! CHECK! CHECK!" through a bullhorn directly over my shoulder. Prior to his stint at Tennessee, Majors won a national championship at Pitt in 1976, powered by Heisman Trophy–winning running back Tony Dorsett. Jaynes brought Majors back to Pittsburgh in '92, and he'd connected with Dad in small part because of his relationship with me.

Jaynes continued. "We had Miami in town for a late season game. You know they were really good. They always were. They had just lost in the national championship the year before and had Ray Lewis and those guys, and we were having a really tough season."

It had been a tough season for Dad, too. A few weeks earlier he was in Austin for a game between Pitt and Texas, but received a call in the middle of the night that his mother, Mary Caddell, had passed away. So, when Dad arrived at Pitt, Coach Majors came straight to him to express his condolences. Jaynes was also eager to visit with his old friend, but he joined the conversation carrying a surprise. He had a new grandchild and the baby was at the stadium, so the athletic director got the child, brought it out onto the field, and handed the infant to Dad. The three men and a baby were talking, laughing, and catching up.

"All of the sudden," Jaynes recalls, "We hear someone yell, 'Well, what the hell is this?!'"

It was Butch Davis, head coach of the Miami Hurricanes, who had walked out of the locker room for a road game against the Pittsburgh Panthers and the first thing he'd seen was a referee, in uniform, holding the grandbaby of the smiling Pitt athletic director, and with the arm of the Pitt head coach draped over his black and white striped shoulders. Dad handed the baby back as quickly as he could, Jaynes and Majors laughing.

"Butch wasn't actually worried about it. At the end of the day, coaches and officials are all in it together on Saturdays. There aren't a whole lot of people who really understand what that's really like. So, the ones that do, especially the ones who have been around for a long time, they can't help but end up becoming friends. And the good ones all understand that just because you might be friends, that doesn't mean you're getting favors once the game starts."

Oval Jaynes laughs.

"Okay, not all of them are friends. But we always have been."

Chapter 3

Home Games

M Y FIRST REAL MEMORY of Dad as a college football
official isn't from a stadium or a practice field. It's from
a PTA meeting at my elementary school in Shelby, North Carolina. I was in the third grade. Dad was the PTA president
(because, you know, he didn't already have enough to do), and
I distinctly remember watching him crossing the gymnasium
stage to take his place behind the podium and address whatever it is that PTA presidents must address. That journey to
that podium was perilous, not because of any overly angry
parents or teachers, but because he was on crutches. I remember being very nervous about that. I wasn't alone.

Sam McGee

My first memory is pretty much the same, but it wasn't at
school. I remember Dad in our basement den, with his right
foot stuck in a bucket of ice. I remember him explaining to
me what had happened and why he was having to sit there
and basically torture himself.

I was, what, six years old? I didn't like that at all.

It dawns on me that this is the first time you are really meeting my brother, Sam. Today, he is a hugely successful attorney, representing good, hardworking people when they find themselves thrust into extraordinarily awful situations, hard times often unleashed upon them by cold, uncaring corporations. Sam has dedicated his life to forcing those who don't care to care.

No one will make you laugh harder than Sam McGee, but no one will ever work harder than Sam McGee. His intensity is matched only by his heart. That's what makes him a good lawyer, father, and man. If you'd met him when he was six, none of what he's done or what you will read from him in this book would surprise you. The same skills of observation and research that he used to graduate from Yale Law and now uses to prepare for court are how he has always attacked every aspect of his life. That certainly includes how he studied every bit of Dad's officiating career, from the execution of rule enforcement and mechanics on Saturday afternoons to, unfortunately, the injuries that sometimes got in the way of completing those tasks.

It was one of those injuries here in 1979 that had Dad's right foot swollen like a water balloon, stuffed in that ice bucket at home and into a walking cast at my school's PTA meeting. The Saturday before he'd been officiating a Week 2 game between Carson–Newman and Wofford. He was a line judge and had been given a heads up that someone from the ACC would be watching the game, scouting him as a potential NCAA Division I official.

Dad

I wasn't nervous about that, because I was happy where I was. If they called, great. If they didn't, okay. But I absolutely wanted to make sure that I showed them my best effort, no matter what might happen.

During one of the game's very first plays, he ran in from the sideline to spot the ball. Bodies were still rolling and crashing at the end of the play when he arrived and a giant Carson–Newman lineman jumped into the air to keep from tripping over all those bodies on the ground. He landed right on top of Dad, dragging his cleat down Dad's right shin, into the top of his right foot, trapping his ankle and twisting it badly. Dad toughed it out until halftime, when he went in to see the Wofford trainer, who started unlacing the right shoe and then suddenly stopped. He told Dad that if he kept going and pulled that shoe off, they'd never get it back on because his ankle was already so swollen. Instead, the trainer wrapped the entire shoe in athletic tape and sent Dad back out to work the second half. When the game was over and Dad finally pulled off his cleats and socks, his shin was crusted with blood and his ankle was twice its normal size.

The next morning, when Mom pulled back the sheets on the bed, Dad's ankle was so swollen that she gasped.

Dad

If I hadn't had toenails you wouldn't have even known it was a foot.

That Tuesday we got my evaluation from the ACC observer who'd come to see the game. He provided all of this detailed criticism of the other officials he'd been there to see. Next to my name he wrote one sentence.

"Ran like he was hurt."

Over the long haul, that right ankle became an unforeseen blessing. Dad never again worked a game when he didn't have that ankle taped by the athletic training staff of the home team. He would knock on the door a couple of hours before kickoff, and they would always oblige. He was usually not alone, as other officials were also nursing injuries, from bum hamstrings to bone spurs. The unexpected benefit of those times spent on the trainers' tables was the chance to visit with the players who were there to have an injury prepped and the coaches who were stopping by to check on those players.

Dad

It always caught people off guard the first time they saw it, a grey-headed guy in his black and white uniform getting taped up. But I made real friendships in those rooms. Some of those legendary trainers taped my right ankle for 30 years. Coaches would stop by to chat. The legendary former players you always see in the stadium on game days, they would talk your ears off. We even met Lee Greenwood in the trainer's room.

Joe Paterno thought it was hilarious. The first time I went to Penn State, he came in there and saw me and couldn't stop talking about it. "Look at this! This guy is so serious about this, he's getting taped up! You got any eligibility left? A man your age that is this intense, I could use some of that!"

Paterno joked, but he was also a regular on the training table, thanks to a series of injuries in the 2000s, everything from a broken leg suffered in a sideline collision versus Wisconsin to a self-inflicted hip injury while demonstrating an onside kick. A painful reminder that only the players are wearing pads and helmets.

But before all of that came this PTA meeting at my elementary school. I've never forgotten it because I've also never forgotten my mother's assessment of the situation, which is was almost as short and every bit as memorable as that ACC officiating evaluator. She had driven us to the meeting, helped Dad out of the car, handed him his crutches, and run interference for him when too many people came running up with a sympathetic but nosey, "Oh, Jerry! What happened?!"

Now, as he hobbled up to the podium with his presidential notes, Mom leaned over to me and whispered, only half-joking. "Let's say a little prayer that Dad doesn't fall off the stage right now."

Dad

People will ask me, 'Well, how did Hannah feel about you officiating?" or "How did Hannah balance everything at home with two boys and her work and all of that when you were gone every weekend doing games?"

The answer is that she did it so well it was never an issue. At least, it never felt like an issue. She knew that I loved it. It gave us opportunities that we wouldn't have had without it. And honestly, it was just always there. I started working high school games almost as soon as we were married and I worked college games for the rest of her life.

Hannah Covington of Rockingham, North Carolina, was never one to be described as a big-time sports fan, but that certainly didn't mean she wasn't around games her entire life. From the time she cheered on the sidelines of the Rockingham High Rockets all the way to watching from the stands of America's most hallowed football grounds, featuring field judge Dr. Jerry McGee, she was never far from a football playing field.

Mom grew up in the Cartledge Creek community well beyond the outskirts of Rockingham, a country crossroads that made Dad's textile mill neighborhoods look like Manhattan.

My parents met in the hallways of school, the three-sport athlete and cheerleader who was two years his junior. They dated on and off, all the while somehow knowing in the backs of their minds that were destined to be together, even as young Jerry left for college and shortly thereafter young Hannah went west to California to be with her older sister and also start college.

By the time Dad graduated from East Carolina, Mom was back in Rockingham and they were married on August 15, 1965. One year later, he received the call from Mr. Gaddy about the possibility of officiating high school games. Mom and Dad sensed an immediate opportunity. She hadn't been able to continue with school and was working as a librarian in Rockingham. So, they made the decision that whatever money Dad made from officiating would go straight toward paying Mom's tuition. She was going back to college.

When she graduated from Pembroke State (now UNC Pembroke) with her education degree, she was pregnant with me. I was born on November 2, a Monday, and Dad worked high school games on the Friday nights before and after. Sam was born three years later, somewhere in between two of the five games Dad worked during his second season in small college football.

My mother was smart, sweet, and funny, and she had a Jedi mind trick ability to influence an entire room full of people without those people realizing it. She was five-foot-nothing, built from equal parts heart and, when she needed it, dynamite.

The story goes that one night after Sam and I had grown up and moved out, Mom and Dad stopped at a gas station somewhere in rural North Carolina. While Dad was filling up the car, he pointed out a very rough-looking redneck exiting the convenience store. He joked to Mom, "Just think, you could have ended up married to that guy."

Mom, not missing a beat, replied, "Yep. And he'd be a university president and would have just refereed the Rose Bowl."

Dad

When Mr. Gaddy first called me, he was a guy Hannah and I both knew. He was the father-in-law of one our best friends from high school. A lot of the officials who were already working with him were longtime friends of ours, too.

When he offered me the chance, I said to Hannah that if I was going to do this, then I was going to do it all out. I was going to take every assignment offered to me, even that first year of high school when I had to work five games for free. And from 1966 through 2009, I turned down exactly one game, and that wasn't until the later half of my career.

She never questioned that plan. Not even once. Even as what started as a Friday night hobby turned into airplane travel and longer weekends. There were moments where it was tough, for sure. But Hannah always made it work. Always.

She made it work so well, in fact, that as little kids Sam and I honestly don't remember him ever being gone. Our lives at home hummed along so normally that it never felt any different. So, no, we don't have a lot of memories of Dad as an official during the high school and small college days, aside from snapshot mental images and an immense sense of pride.

During our time in Rockingham, when I was no more than a few years old, I distinctly remember seeing Dad in his black and white uniform, jumping into the car and leaving for games at local schools. Our neighbor across the street was Earl Yates, a former Duke offensive lineman, who was also a high school official. His daughter, Amy, was my best friend. On Friday afternoons, Amy and I would sit on our tricycles and watch our fathers leave for games. Sometimes they would leave together. Other times, they would leave at the same time, but headed to different destinations. Then there were the times that a carload of other guys would stop to pick up my dad and Amy's dad, everyone with their uniforms in hand.

So, as far as I knew in my little world, everyone's father did this, right?

Sam

I do have small college football memories from when we were at Gardner–Webb, but Dad wasn't there for them. He was off working a game of his own, so I remember going to games on Saturdays, but just with Mom and Ryan. That's where I think we both started really loving college football.

I remember very clearly walking up to the stadium at Gardner–Webb and seeing a guy running the opening kick-off back for a touchdown. And I remember the final score of that game. It was 84–0. They were playing Mexico. Not New Mexico or New Mexico State. Mexico.

I remember those games, too. But my memories mostly involve playing tackle football behind the little concession stand as the real games were happening nearby, tossing a little black-and-red plastic football, given away by a local car dealer, and mercilessly hitting the other sons of the Gardner–Webb coaches and staff.

No matter where we were, no one had any doubts that we were the sons of Jerry McGee, the ref. Because my brother proudly wore one of Dad's black officiating ballcaps everywhere we went. Seriously. School, dinner, the Grand Canyon, Disneyland, church…when I say everywhere we went, I mean *everywhere we went.*

Sam

I have no idea how it started. Somehow, I picked up one of his old ref hats when I was three, and I wore it for several years straight. I mean that literally. You cannot find a picture of me during that timeframe when I did not have that hat on my head. I changed my Halloween costume to a referee uniform so I could wear the hat. Mom and Dad had to make me take it off when I got into the bathtub, and only then just long enough to wash my hair. I slept in it.

Dad

Like, it was a fight every single night not to wear it to bed. We would finally convince him to take it off and put it on his nightstand. Then later, when we'd check in on him before we went to bed, he would have put it on as soon we left the room and he was fast asleep.

Sam

The pinnacle of the insanity was the year two teachers and a school photographer couldn't make me take the ref hat off for my school picture. The more frustrated they got, the more I dug my heels in. Even my classmates were joining in. "No way!" I still have that class photo of me wearing that worn out old hat. I drew pictures of baseball teams and army units in little notebooks, and all the soldiers and team members are wearing ref hats. I still don't know why. I don't look back on my childhood and see Dad gone; I see him there. But I guess when I was that young, he was on the road a fair bit for work, and we weren't going to his games yet. Maybe I was just proud of him, or it made me feel closer to him. Hell, I don't know. Maybe I just liked the damn hat. What finally ended it? Baseball. I couldn't take the field without wearing the official uniform hat. Guess who the coach was? Dad.

In 1980, Dad left Gardner–Webb for another small college, but in a much larger locale. Meredith College (Go Angels!) was an all-women's school. No football. But it was located in Raleigh, North Carolina, a longtime sleepy capital city that was about to explode with growth. Meredith was surrounded by the sprawling campus of North Carolina State University. Carter–Finley Stadium, home of the NCSU Wolfpack, was just across the highway from the Meredith campus. Only 20 miles to the west sat Kenan Stadium, home of the University of North Carolina Tar Heels, and Wallace Wade Stadium, playing field of the Duke Blue Devils. A little further down I-40 was Groves Stadium, home of the Wake Forest Demon Deacons.

We had moved to Tobacco Road, where in 1980 the home teams were playing football games against the likes of Penn State, Oklahoma, South Carolina, Clemson, and Auburn. North Carolina was a top 10 team. NC State had a roster full of future NFL talent. Wake Forest had a hot young coach in John Mackovic. Duke was going against conventional Southern football wisdom and starting to sling the ball all over the field, via plays conjured up in the mind of its brash new offensive coordinator, former Heisman Trophy–winner Steve Spurrier.

This was big-time college football. It was all around us, and it was infectious.

Dad

I finished my doctorate (in education) in September of '79. I accepted the job in Raleigh that December, moving in

January. Right after that, I got a letter from the ACC office in Greensboro, from Mr. Neve, wanting to know if I would be interested in starting the process of becoming part of the officiating group of the ACC.

Here I was, moving right into the middle of the conference, right on the road with four of the schools and within driving distance of a handful of others. Timing, right?

Dad would still work a small college schedule, but now he would mix in trips to junior colleges, places where ACC schools sent their freshman and JV teams. That meant there would be evaluations from ACC coaches and film that Mr. Neve could watch.

But the best part of the new arrangement was a direct result of the league's conflict of interest rules.

Because we lived in Raleigh, Dad was not allowed to officiate NC State games. But because we lived in Raleigh, he would also be called upon to work as many NC State scrimmages and practices as he could, spring, summer, and fall. For Dad, that was big news because it meant reps. He could see real live Division I football players in action, over and over again. And in the more relaxed atmosphere of practice, he could also quiz coaches on rules and situations, while they did the same with him.

But most importantly, all of those scrimmages meant my little brother and I got full access and pretty much free reign to roam a genuine college football stadium. At Gardner–Webb, we'd played with a plastic mini football with other kids outside a stadium that sat a few hundred people. At NC State, we were playing with a real football on a grass hill that overlooked the end zone of Carter–Finley Stadium that sat 47,000, while a team scrimmaged below us, preparing to take on South Carolina or Miami.

Sam

We were on the sideline, meeting guys who were headed to the NFL. When we first got there, Mike Quick was on that team. He went on to be a key wide receiver for the Philadelphia Eagles for years. I think he should be in the Pro Football Hall of Fame. But here we are, standing in the middle of their practices, and they didn't care! I was just struck by the speed and the violence of it all. I was seven, eight years old when we first started going out there.

Thanks to that time I have also always known why Gatorade has dominated the sports drink market. Back then there were only two choices, and State used No. 2. It tasted like swill. I know that because they let me drink it all the time. And I have also always known why every level of football ended up banning Stickum, the sticky stuff players used to put on their hands to help catch the ball. I watched those guys just slather that stuff all over themselves. It was like brown goo and it got all over everything. There would be empty packets of it all over the ground on the sideline at NC State.

Sam was drawn to the duties of ball boy, an art he would perfect over the years, including a role with a national championship–winning football team. I was immediately drawn to the local media who were there to cover those scrimmages, particularly the TV reporters and newspaper photographers. I would follow them around, not to try and sneak onto television, but to observe how they did their jobs. I even managed to sneak into the Carter–Finley Stadium press box one night, only to have a security guard grab me by the arm. When he angrily asked, "Where are you parents?!" I sheepishly pointed down to the playing field.

The head coach of the Wolfpack was Monte Kiffin. Today, he is renowned as a defensive innovator, inventor of the "Tampa 2" cover defense that won Super Bowl XXXVII for the Tampa Bay Buccaneers and has been mimicked throughout football ever since. But in 1980, he was known as a funny, somewhat eccentric first-time head coach. Some days he would show up for practice in a Hawaiian shirt. One day he waited until the entire was team dressed in uniform and shoulder pads and walked out in a swimsuit to announce that it was too damn hot, screw practice, they were going to the swimming pool.

When Sam and I would play those pickup games in Carter–Finley, we would play with and against the sons of Kiffin's coaching staff. There was one of those boys in particular we came to loathe. He was younger than Sam, not more than five or six, and in the middle of our impromptu games on the steep, grassy hill he was constantly insisting that he was being held or that someone had committed pass interference or that someone was running the wrong receiving route.

One evening, the kid got so loud that Monte Kiffin ran the length of the field, blowing his whistle and screaming in front of everyone in attendance, *"Dammit, Lane! Stop crying! You're messing up our whole damn practice!"*

Sam

As the years went by, I had forgotten about those pickup games in the stadium. Then one day I was watching ESPN and they were reporting a guy named Lane Kiffin had just been named the youngest head coach in NFL history.

I immediately called Ryan. "Is that little mouthy kid from NC State now the head coach of the freaking Oakland Raiders?!"

When we weren't fighting with future head coaches, we were watching Dad learn about the next level of football, and we were learning with him. When we weren't with him at NC State, we might be with him working scrimmages at Duke or UNC. When there were no scrimmages to work, we would watch him study the rules changes for the upcoming season. He would have his little yellow NCAA rules book in hand at home, by the neighborhood swimming pool, or on the beach. Every flat surface in our house seemed to have some sort of rules papers on it, lessons and quizzes, easily identified by diagrammed football plays and these old, goofy, clip art cartoon football players and officials that were used to decorate otherwise boring breakdown of rules and on-field mechanics. They still use those cartoons.

After Dad felt like he was sufficiently schooled on any new rule, that's when his in–living room demonstrations would break out. I might be lined up at wide receiver, Sam at cornerback, and Mom at free safety, being moved around the room by Dad like we were action figures as he explained the difference between pass interference or a no-call, in bounds or out of bounds, and catch versus no-catch.

Every morning before work, Dad would lace on his running shoes and log laps at my middle school. After I made the track team at that same middle school, I'd run with him. Many afternoons in-season, we wouldn't know that he was yet home from work and thus be surprised when we saw him running 30-yard wind sprints in the yard…backward. It worried the neighbors to death. But hey, that's how downfield officials run.

As goofy as Monte Kiffin could be, he was also still a serious football man. Dad was merely one of a large group of college officials who lived in Raleigh, and Kiffin loved to bring them in to talk to his coaches and players about rules, new and old, and what an official was or wasn't looking for to enforce those rules.

Dad

People don't realize this, but when you see a head coach and a veteran official discussing a play during a game, a lot of times that's a continuation of a conversation they've already been having for a long time. It might go back to a practice or a scrimmage or a meeting with the team, or a discussion at a summer conference officiating meeting. A lot of coaches would show up at the officials' annual offseason clinic to listen in on what we're talking about and see if they can learn something or explain something to us.

It is perhaps the least-known aspect of an already widely misunderstood profession, the relationships between officials and coaches, especially veterans on both sides. See: Dad holding a baby on the sideline at Pitt.

In some cases, that extends to groups of players as well, particularly if an official resides in that area and works a lot of scrimmages at a certain school, or has worked a lot of games with one team during a particular player or coach's tenure.

Dad

I mentioned I like to remind people that officials are humans. They hurt and they make mistakes, just like other humans. Well, it's easy to forget that coaches are human, too.

I remember one day I was in the locker room at NC State getting dressed and Monte Kiffin just walked in and sat down. He said to me, "Man, I really hope this works. I hope I can do this. I've always wanted to be a head coach. I love this place. My family loves Raleigh. We just had another son. I really, really hope this works out."

A year later, with a three-season record of 16–17, Monte Kiffin was fired. As we know now, he would go on to have a legendary career—but as an assistant coach. He would never be a head coach again.

The big leagues of college football, they are an unforgiving place. It's a fact of football life with which Dad was about to become very familiar. After two seasons under the ACC microscope, he'd passed his tests, both the rules exams and the eye tests of the Mr. Neve and his evaluators. In 1982, he'd be working at least a few ACC games.

I was a preteen and Sam was about to hit double-digits. Our school and after-school schedules were moving into overdrive. Mom was teaching elementary school and carting us from one end of Raleigh to the other. It was a lot to handle, and it was only going to get worse. So, Dad went to her and they talked. When he'd made the move to small college, the only real change in that routine was everything took place on Saturday instead of Friday and instead of getting home at 1:00 AM Saturday mornings he got home at the same time Sunday mornings. But now, if he did his job and did it right…if this actually worked…it would mean airplanes and overnights and at least another 10 nights per year away, added to his already-growing weeknight travel schedule as a fundraiser for Meredith College.

Dad

Again, Hannah never hesitated. She would make it work. She always did.

Now Dad needed to make it work on Saturday afternoons in the Atlantic Coast Conference.

Coaches' Timeout
with Monte and Lane Kiffin

"Hey, son, come here! I need you to retell that story you told me earlier!"

It is November 18, 2017, in Boca Raton, Florida. The Florida Atlantic University Owls have just boat-raced their archrival, the Florida International University Panthers, 52–24 in the game known as the Shula Bowl. The head coach at FAU is Lane Kiffin. His offensive coordinator is his little brother, Chris. Listed on the staff as a "defensive assistant" is his father, Monte.

It is Monte Kiffin who calls out to me now, after the ball-game and the ensuing celebration has wound down. Prior to the game, in the modest FAU Stadium press box, I had spotted the living legend grabbing a snack while the Owls went through their pregame warmups down on the field. I told him that we had met before, when we both much younger, at NC State. He smiled and said, "Those were good days. But I had no idea what I was doing."

I recounted the story of the hotheaded little boy who blew up the pickup football games on the Carter–Finley Stadium hill—his little boy. The little boy who had become the man who had become the head coach of the Raiders, Tennessee, USC, FAU, and, a couple of years from this moment, Ole Miss. The very stadium tower in which I now talked to Lane Kiffin's father was decorated with a giant banner of Lane Kiffin's face, designed to catch the eye of people traveling on the nearby Interstate.

Monte Kiffin did a spit take with his coffee when I recalled how he had stopped practice to tell the kid to chill out. "Hell, he hasn't changed much, has he?"

A few hours later, the father calls me over to tell the story again, this time to his son. Lane Kiffin, without so much as a hint of a smile, looks me in the eye for the first time since we played those games in that stadium grass while our fathers worked on their games on the playing field below.

"Your dad is a referee. Then you know the truth here. If you guys hadn't kept committing all those penalties, we could have actually had some fun."

CHAPTER 4

YEA, THOUGH I WALK THROUGH THE VALLEY OF THE SHADOW OF DEATH

D AD'S FIRST GAME in Division I-A—what we now call the Football Bowl Subdivision (FBS)—was the Division I-A/FBS equivalent of his first small college game, Emory & Henry at Guilford.

The visiting James Madison Dukes would one day become a I-AA (Football Championship Subdivision, or FCS) power-house. But September 18, 1982 was not that day, even with future Washington Redskins hero Gary Clark catching passes. The home team Virginia Cavaliers would one day become a perennial ACC title contender and bowl season regular. But this was also not that day, even with future College Foot-ball Hall of Fame coach George Welsh at the helm. It was only Welsh's second game in Charlottesville, hired from the U.S. Naval Academy to try and awaken the long-dormant UVA program. But he'd already lost in Week 1 to his former employer and on his way to an inaugural campaign that would end with a 2–9 record.

Never one for extended jovial moods, the former Navy quarterback and Joe Paterno apprentice was of particularly bad temperament on this afternoon. His demeanor did not improve as James Madison pushed toward a 21–17 upset win.

Dad

I was a back judge, and again, I was nervous. I wasn't nervous because of the game or even because Mr. Neve was going to be there to evaluate me in person. I was nervous because I was subbing for my hero, a man named Bob Sandell, who was the model of consistency for downfield officials. He was already a legend and is still my all-time favorite football official. But he was from Charlottesville, so he couldn't work Virginia games.

I was plugged into a team of real veteran guys. The referee was Bob Cooper, who had a long career as a college football and lacrosse official. The umpire was Bradley Faircloth, who would go on to succeed Mr. Neve as the conference coordinator. Charlie Neely was head linesman; Bill Luper was the field judge. Bo Menton, who was a dentist during the week, was the line judge and, like Sandell, he was already a living legend among college officials. It was a ridiculously great crew and they really worked hard to make sure that I felt comfortable.

But these guys had worked hundreds of ACC games. I had worked zero. So, when George Welsh looked out there, he knew who all of these other guys were, but I know he was wondering, *Now, who the hell is this guy?*

Dad was working hard to play it cool, but in reality, he was just trying to get comfortable in his own shoes. Like, literally. He'd never been on artificial turf before.

Dad

The first punt of my first ACC game, the punter shanked it out of bounds. What happens on that play is that the referee is with the kicker, so he follows the ball through the air and he lines it up where it goes out of bounds. My job is to raise my hand and run along the sideline where it went out. If it rolls out of bounds, I can see it and I mark it. But in the air, that's on the referee. So, I run along and when I get the signal from the white hat, I mark where the ball went out of bounds and we set up for the line of scrimmage for the next series.

Now I'm running up the sideline, just textbook. But I look for Cooper and he's gone. He's running down the field. He hadn't thought for one second about me. Totally out of a character for a great official. It happens. As I was looking at him, like, what the hell, man, he realized what he had done. So, as he was running, he kind of gave me a half-assed little point with his hand, like, "Yeah, right there somewhere..." So, all I can do is make my best guess, mark the spot, and signal timeout. George Welsh went crazy. I wasn't within five yards of the correct spot. But I didn't know that. I am literally guessing. And now, for the rest of the game, I'm thinking, "Well, the ACC was fun..."

When the game was over, Mr. Neve was going over our evaluation with us in the locker room. He says, "McGee, what happened on that punt?" Well, I'm not going to throw Bob Cooper under the bus. I'm a rookie. I'm going to take one for the team.

"Mr. Neve, I didn't get a great start on the kick, so running down the field I had to make my best guess on that spot."

Mr. Neve, who was always a very serious guy, said, "Yeah, I could tell you were guessing." Well, that felt pretty awful. I hadn't really messed anything up, but now, officially at least, I had. Or, so I though. Then he turned and looked at Cooper. "Bob, the reason he was f--king guessing is because that was your call!"

Bob looked at me and said, "Yeah, I know..." He wasn't ever going to let me take the fall, certainly not in my first game. But he appreciated that I was willing to take the fall for him.

That night, Norval Neve gave Dad a piece of advice that he would repeat so many times over the next two seasons and has reverberated in Dad's mind ever since.

Dad

Mr. Neve said over and over again, "Let your mind digest what your eyes have just seen."

He warned us to not to call anything too soon. That was just inviting trouble. You see a play and you immediately want to run in and call it. Or something gets sideways, like that kick at Virginia, and you have this need to fix it immediately. But there's nothing wrong with taking a breath, processing what you've seen, and then making the call.

People will yell, "Man, that was a late flag!" or "What took him so long to signal touchdown?" But Mr. Neve would tell us, "There's no such thing as a late flag. That's an official taking a breath and making sure of what he is about to do."

Virginia's Scott Stadium is a beautiful facility, one of the nation's most underrated college football stadiums, lined with columns that blend it in with Thomas Jefferson's practically perfect college campus. And when the team is good—and Dad would go on to work some incredible games there, perhaps the greatest in ACC history—the UVA crowd has always had the ability to be raucous when the moment inspires them to do so.

But it isn't Death Valley. That was the location of Dad's second-ever ACC game and his first full-fledged conference game. It was October 16, 1982, and Clemson was hosting Duke. The Tigers were the defending national champions and ranked 20th after a season-opening 13–7 loss to Herschel Walker and Georgia. But now Clemson was rolling, and they were angry. They were on probation for recruiting violations, kept off of television and out any postseason bowl for two years. The weekend before this game, they'd defeated Virginia 48–0. That same day, Dad, still working a full South Atlantic Conference schedule, had officiated a game at Catawba College. There were about 500 people at the game.

For this afternoon contest against the Blue Devils, there were 62,822 Clemson fans in attendance, in a soaring double-decker concrete facility, packed to the sky with orange. At one end of the stadium, just-unveiled lettering read 1989 NATIONAL CHAMPIONS. At the other end, also known as The Hill, as the Tigers entered the stadium to rush down that hill, they paused to slap their gloved hands against a desert rock mounted atop a podium for good luck. In 1945, after watching his team get bulldozed by Clemson 76–0, Presbyterian College Blue Hose head coach Lonnie McMillan compared the misery of the experience to a visit he'd made to Death Valley, California, a decade earlier. In the 1960s, a Clemson alum driving across that same desert picked up a small boulder and delivered it to legendary Clemson head coach Frank Howard. When Howard tried to have it thrown away, a staffer instead had it placed atop an altar that overlooked the new Death Valley.

So, as has happened every autumn Saturday afternoon since, the Tigers stampeded down The Hill, past the concrete slab inscribed "From Death Valley, CA to Death Valley, SC" and onto the playing field below, as the Tiger Band played the Tiger Rag...and hundreds of orange and white balloons were unleashed into the skies of Upstate South Carolina... and gracious sakes alive and glory be, this here, this was a different college football world.

Dad

We drove in, and every road was covered in orange tiger paws. Every one of them. We got to the locker room and it was huge, like a walk-in closet. Our names were engraved on these orange nameplates over our locker. There was a giant fruit basket, a box full of shaving supplies, a huge meal waiting on us. I've never seen so much fried chicken. And then the pregame. I had never seen anything like it.

Sam

If I have an earliest memory of Dad working an actual ACC game, it was this one. I don't think I even really knew who Clemson had played. I just knew that he had been to Clemson for the first time, because when he got home, he talked about the size of it. I remember him telling us about all the orange vehicles. Orange vans and orange Cadillacs with tiger tails hanging out of the trunks. He gave us the stuff they'd given him. He was so excited. What he kept saying was, "Guys, we think we've seen big-time college football. But now I've really seen it. This is a whole new ballgame."

Dad

To be clear here, all of that was cool. But as soon as the game started all of that atmosphere and tradition, that was gone from my mind. It was time to go to work. And we had to go to work just about as soon as the game started. Right off the bat we had a really bizarre call on the field. I'm on the sideline right in the front the bench, so as always, I'm the guy who has to explain to the head coach, and the head coach was Danny Ford.

Okay, if you don't already know about Danny Ford, you really need to, because this is not the last time he will be mentioned in this book. Honestly, we could write an entire compilation of only Danny Ford stories. The reason for that is the man himself. A native of Gadsden, Alabama, Ford played for Bear Bryant at Alabama in the late 1960s and then joined the Crimson Tide staff as an assistant coach. In 1977 he joined the staff at Clemson as offensive line coach under another Bryant disciple, Charley Pell. When Pell left for Florida in '78, Ford was named head coach. His first game as head coach was the 1978 Gator Bowl. It's one of the most infamous games in college football history, when enraged Ohio State head coach Woody Hayes suddenly punched a Clemson player on the sideline and was fired the following day. Only three seasons later, the Tigers won their first national championship. So, to be clear to you youngsters out there, Dabo Swinney didn't turn Clemson into a college football powerhouse. He returned it to the promise it had once shown under Danny Ford.

Ford was the Mr. Gaddy of college football coaches. He was never without a wad of tobacco jammed into his cheeks.

He liked to crouch along the sideline and pick blades of grass out of the turf. He wore mesh-back trucker hats and when he wanted people to know that he wasn't happy, he would poke the bill of that cap with one finger and push it until it was mounted high atop the back half of his head. When Danny Ford talks, it sounds like a tuning fork being played with a chunk of gravel.

Danny Ford was—still is—a folksy quote machine. He once assessed a Clemson player's performance by saying, "He looks like Tarzan, but plays like Jane." He once said to a group of reporters, "I don't know why y'all come to my practices. I don't come to your office and watch you type." And when someone tried to overcomplicate a football observation, he replied, "It don't take a scientific rocket to figure this out."

Dad

My first ever interaction with Danny was in this Duke game and on a really goofy play. The Duke quarterback ran about 25 yards, and as he was getting hit, he threw the ball to a teammate, and threw it forward. The guy didn't catch it, it hit the ground, and a Clemson player fell on it. The place went crazy. They thought they'd recovered a fumble.

But because the quarterback was way downfield, what we had was an illegal forward pass—an *incomplete* illegal forward pass. Clemson's only option was to take a five-yard penalty.

I'm the sideline guy, so Ford says to me, "I don't want to take this damn penalty. I want the damn football." I started trying to explain why he couldn't do that and exactly what happened, and I was doing a really terrible job of it. Danny started yelling, "That wasn't no damn forward pass!" The white hat was a veteran guy, Jimmy Knight, and he saw me struggling.

He ran over and calmed Danny down and explained it way better than I had. Danny said, "You mean we are going to get the ball." Jimmy explained, no, Duke was *keeping* the ball.

We're done and I was walking back to my position and Danny said to me, "Hey! You ain't never been down here, have you?" I said, "No sir, I have not."

Danny Ford said to me, "Well, this ain't f--king Catawba."

He was certainly right about that.

Like all things pertaining to Ford, it was also sneaky smart. The coach could have made his point by throwing out the name of any small college anywhere, but he had done his research. He knew that Dad had indeed worked at Catawba the week before, so that was specifically the school that he mentioned.

Danny Ford always did his research. During the eight years Dad and Ford were in the ACC together, Ford always made sure his entire coaching staff attended the conference's annual offseason officiating clinic. These were the meetings where officials went over rules changes, watched film, and took the written and physical exams that went toward their grades as officials, their ranking among others at their position, and largely determined what their regular season schedule would be a well as their chances of earning a bowl trip at the end of that season.

There were always coaches from various ACC schools at the clinic, but Ford and his group were the only ones guaranteed to show up every single year. In the conference rooms where rules discussions were taking place, a Clemson coach was there to ask questions. In the hallway, at lunch, you name a spot in the meeting space or at the hotel and Ford and his guys were there, asking questions about what they could and couldn't get away with. And yes, that included the bar.

> **Dad**
>
> One year we had the summer clinic in Charlottesville and the word got out on a particular night that the beer was in my room, where I was staying with my longtime crewmate, Bill Booker.

We also need to take a moment here and introduce you to the great William Booker of Lynchburg, Virginia. First of all, no one calls him William. Second of all, no one calls him Bill, either. He's just Booker.

Booker is big man with an even bigger laugh, and I'm not sure that anyone loves sports more than he does. A former multi-sport star at Ferrum and Lynchburg Colleges, he was the son of a minor league baseball player who became one himself, an infielder in the Houston Colt .45s organization (now the Astros). Booker then became a legendary Virginia high school coach in baseball, football, and basketball. He also officiated seemingly 365 days a year, from Virginia prep sports to college football and basketball. Like my Dad, Booker loved his father, his coaches, and he took great joy in including his family in his officiating experience, especially his three sons. The McGee and Booker boys got to know each other sitting in the officials' family ticket rows or in vans being hauled around during bowl game trips.

Booker and McGee, the line judge and the field judge, began sharing the same sideline in 1986 and continued to do so for the next half-decade in the ACC, a season in the Big

East, and then a second ACC stanza after that. They always roomed together. Everyone knew that no one worked harder than Booker and McGee. But everyone also knew no one had more fun than Booker and McGee.

Dad

Sure enough, everyone at this rules clinic ended up in our hotel room. Danny Ford and his staff were in there, along with a few other coaches and about 10 other ACC officials. Danny started talking about a play from the season before. He didn't like the penalty that was called on that play.

It was getting late and he had enjoyed some adult beverages. He got real demonstrative as he stood up and was walking through the play. "What you called was this...but what really happened on the play was..." and then he tripped over his own feet and, *wham!*, crashed right through the little table in the middle of the room. He broke all four legs off it. He hit so hard they shot off in four different directions. Well, he popped right up and we all laughed and decided to call it a night. We had our big rules exam the next morning, and we needed to sleep.

Booker and I got into our beds and in the dark, I said to him, "Damn, man, we're going to have to pay for that table." He said he'd talk to the manager and we went on to sleep.

About two or three o'clock in the morning, there was a knock at the door. Woke us both up. We opened the door, expecting that the manager had heard about what happened and we were about to get chewed out. Instead, this really young Clemson assistant coach walks in with another table under his arm. He set it down, picked up the pieces of the old table, said "See you later, boys," and left.

From sideline chats at scrimmages to chance meetings at airports to, yes, inebriated play demonstrations at rules clinics, the discussion between coaches and officials about what is and isn't allowed within the rules never ends. It's only the screaming part on Saturday afternoons that is televised.

Dad

A few years after I had retired as an official, I was working as president at Wingate University when my phone rang. It was Eric Mele, who had been an assistant at Wingate, but was now the running backs coach at Washington State. He said, "Hey Doc, I've got someone here with a rules question for you..." The next voice I heard was pretty unmistakable. It was Mike Leach. He's the Air Raid guru, so he's always trying to figure out how to get as many players downfield as potential receivers he possibly can. He was wondering about a play he thought might take advantage of some grey area in the rulebook. I can't remember exactly what he asked, but it involved a bizarre snap and, basically, he was trying to find a way to hide one of his receivers on the field. I do remember that it was pretty genius. But it was also 100 percent illegal.

So, here was Mike Leach, a coach I had never met in my life, calling me, a retired field judge, about a cockamamie play he was drawing up in the middle of May, five months since he'd coached his last game and four months before his next one. And what's he doing? Looking for any competitive edge he can find.

It brings to mind another Danny Ford-ism: "All I want is a fair advantage."

Throughout Dad's officiating career, he never saw anyone overtly trying to cheat. Well, nothing super blatant, anyway. Let's just say the 2015 Deflategate controversy involving Tom Brady and the New England Patriots wasn't exactly an original idea. Among the long list of a college officiating crew's pregame duties is to inspect the bags of game balls each team will use in that day's contest. Growing up, on those occasions when my brother and I were allowed in the officials' locker room before games, we'd walk in to find everyone sitting on benches rubbing and squeezing footballs like they were searching for the freshest cantaloupes in the supermarket produce section. Balls that passed the psi test (a number that has moved up and down as the years have gone by) were sent back to the teams. But when equipment managers started getting too antsy about getting those balls back as early as possible, officials started noticing a lot of varying shapes and sizes of those balls when they reappeared after kickoff. So, they stopped giving the post-inspection footballs back to the teams until as close to game time as possible.

Dad

I always admired the people who cared enough to try and get an edge. They weren't cheating. They were playing the game all-out, all the time. When Bobby Bowden was the head coach at Florida State, they would rack up personal fouls for late hits, but he would argue to us that those hits were at the whistle, not after it. He'd tell me, "Jerry, we coach our guys to play to the end of the whistle." They weren't trying to break the rules. They were trying to get every inch they could within those rules.

The greatest teams I saw a lot, like those Florida State teams, or Miami, or Clemson, would even try to gain an inch in how they lined up. When Tommy Tuberville was coaching those great defensive units at Miami in the late 1980s and early '90s, he told me that their goal was to reestablish the line of scrimmage back two yards on every single play. So, before the play their guys would crowd the line of scrimmage as far as they could. If they got flagged, then from there on it was, "Okay, this is where the line is."

The really great teams look for those lines everywhere. You go back and look at the teams I officiated that won championships, and they were usually also the teams that led the league in penalties. The teams who lost games they shouldn't have, they had a lot of fouls of complacency, just being sloppy. The teams that won those games had a lot of fouls of aggression and creativity. And that creativity isn't limited to those 60 minutes on the game clock.

A coach walked up to me during pregame and said, "Jerry, I'm so glad you're here today. Look at that right cornerback for those guys. He's good. But he holds all the time, but I know you'll get it." I'm not going to call that kid for holding just because a coach told me to. It isn't going to sway my judgment during a game. But in that coach's mind, he's just earned an advantage. It makes him feel good. That's a competitor who never stops. Like Danny Ford letting me know he knew where I worked the weekend before. I know how he knew. He had a guy on his sideline who'd seen me at Catawba. But that's homework. That's someone looking for an edge.

That's the mentality behind those nice lockers, fruit baskets, and personalized orange nameplates. Someone in Clemson's athletic department was thinking, *You know, just maybe, if these guys know how well we take care of them down here at Death Valley, it'll help us out when the time comes.* Did Dad ever pause before throwing his flag against Clemson and think, *I'm not going to call pass interference here today because, man, that fried chicken they gave us after the Duke game was so freaking delicious?* Of course not. But that didn't mean teams and coaches wouldn't keep trying, just in case.

The most memorable case of homework thoroughly done came in what was then the biggest game Dad had worked, the 1990 Orange Bowl between top-ranked Colorado and fourth-ranked Notre Dame. (No, not the one with the Rocket Ismail punt return touchdown that was called back; this was the year before that.) During pregame warmups, Notre Dame head coach Lou Holtz casually walked up to Dad on the sideline. The two had never met, but Holtz threw his arm around the field judge's shoulders like they were old pals and said, "Dr. McGee, how's everything at Furman?" By that time, Dad was in his third year as the VP of Development at Furman University. Then Holtz turned Dad away from the field and pointed into the grandstands of the old Orange Bowl Stadium. "Are Hannah and the boys here? Where are they sitting?"

When the crew gathered in the locker room later, Dad shared his story, and Booker said Holtz had done the same with him, asking about the goings-on in the Lynchburg Public Schools. Everyone on the crew had the same story. Holtz had researched them all, memorized the facts, and casually walked the pregame sidelines to have seven separate *how in the world did he know that?!* conversations with every official in the game.

But back in '82, Dad was still a long way from the Orange Bowl. He was still a rookie in the orange-filled bowl of Death

Valley. Three weeks after the Duke game, he was back at Clemson, this time for a visit from the North Carolina Tar Heels. UNC was ranked 18th and Clemson was 13th. The ACC title was on the line. The game was a total slugfest. Dad's third-ever Division I game, second-ever ACC game, second-ever game at Clemson, and first game between a pair of ranked teams.

And he was afraid he might've screwed the whole thing up.

Dad

I have all the faith in the world in my ability to make calls. I have always believed in my judgment. So, my only concern, just like with Emory & Henry at Guilford 10 years earlier, was just not to do something dumb.

I was at back judge, way downfield from the line of scrimmage. This was a brutal game. It was tied late 13–13. Clemson had the ball and it was driving. I was behind the North Carolina defense. Back then, the only person who counted players on defense was the back judge. That was me. Today, everyone on that end of the field, back judge, side judge, and field judge, all count and check with each other to see that we all are in agreement. At the end of my career, I had counted the defense so many times, 160 times per game for 40 years, that I really could sense when there were 12 men on the field even before I counted—like, "Man, there are too many people out here!" But back then I was a long ways from having any kind of sixth sense. And back then the only person counting was me.

I counted…1-2-3-4-5-6-7-8-9-10-11…and 12. Damn. I counted again. And again. I think I counted seven times. As soon as the ball was snapped, I threw my flag. Instead of running into the middle of the field to report to the referee,

I ran straight toward the sideline to get between Carolina's bench and the field. And the whole time I'm counting again, slow this time. 1...2...3...as deliberately I could do it. But there were definitely 12 out there. As I was explaining it to the referee, a North Carolina guy realized what he'd done and started slinking off. I stopped him and said, "Nope. I need you to stay right there."

My heart was pounding, man. I'm thinking, *If I am wrong here, this will be the shortest tenure in the history of Atlantic Coast Conference officiating.* But I wasn't wrong. The game ended with four straight North Carolina passes into the end zone to try and win it. And I was the only official back there, all those passes coming right at me. Damn baptism by fire. I knew if I could handle that game in that situation, I think I could handle about anything after that.

Those would-be game-winning passes were thrown right at Dad, but also right at *his* dad. Marshall "Pa-Pa" Caddell and my uncle Danny were both there that day, having driven in from Rockingham to take their seat at the 10-yard line, so low in the grandstand that they were nearly on the field.

It meant so much to Dad that they were there. It was a great feeling, but an unfamiliar one. He had so many fantastic father figures in his life, such a great family, but rarely did any of them make it to his games. Coach Eutsler from Rockingham had his own games to coach. Mr. Gaddy and all the boys back in Rockingham had their own games to officiate. But Pa-Pa and Uncle Danny were there on this day, the first of so many games that they would both attend. My father being watched by his father and brother, often with me and my brother sitting alongside, and so many times right there at Clemson.

That day in '82 they had been nervous wrecks watching Dad battle through so many crucial situations in his first real big-time game. That night, they waited for him on the road back into North Carolina to meet for dinner. Uncle Danny asked about something he had noticed during the game, especially during that last frantic series of UNC would-be game-winning passes. He'd seen Dad lined up in the back of the end zone, looking up into the sky and talking to no one in particular. What was he doing?

Dad

I said to him, "I was praying, fool!"

After all, this wasn't f--king Catawba.

Timeout on the ~~Field~~ Red Carpet
with Mike Leach and Gardner Minshew

"Minshew, come here! This is the guy whose Dad told us we couldn't run that play like we wanted to."

It is Thursday night, December 6, 2018, at the College Football Hall of Fame in Atlanta. I am working as a red-carpet reporter for the 2018 College Football Awards on ESPN. Washington State head coach Mike Leach has me by the arm and is calling out to his quarterback, Gardner Minshew, there as a finalist for the Davey O'Brien Award given to the nation's best college quarterback.

Leach and Minshew are a comedy team akin to Laurel and Hardy, complete with one goofy mustache. Both men are equipped with a quirkiness that is very much suited for the offense they ran together in Pullman, the imagination-fueled Air Raid.

"No, really," the coach continues, "I was working up some goofy stuff with Coach Mele and we're like, there's no way this is legal, but every official in Pac-12 hates me, so who are we going to call? Mele said, 'I've got a guy and he was a ref forever and he's also a doctor.' I'm thinking, hey, a doctor, this guy is smart. But then Mele says he's also a college president, so now I'm thinking maybe he isn't so smart. College president feels like the hardest job in the world to me, dealing with all of these people who always need something from you, but then they also all think they can do their job better than you can. So, then I think, well, actually, that sounds a lot like being a college football coach, so let's hear what this referee college president guy has to say."

Minshew looks at me with an expression that says, "Sorry about this, man."

I wink as if to say, "No sweat," and then I add, "Also, Dad went to East Carolina."

The future Jacksonville Jaguars starting quarterback says, "Hey, so did I before I went to Washington State!"

I want to say, "Yes, Gardner Minshew, I know; that's why I told you that." But there's no time. Leach is rolling. He never stopped, even as I was talking to his player.

"So, the play I was asking your dad about, if I remember correctly, was Big Gulp Left, this swinging gate idea, like you sometimes see on special teams, but we wanted to run it out in the open field. Basically, everyone is set up way to the short side of the field, and it looks like a normal formation, but the center doesn't have the ball. The snap is coming from a wide receiver, and he sends it way back over to the quarterback..."

"But," Minshew interrupts, "It doesn't come to me. It goes to the running back lined up next to me. And it also doesn't go to the guy in motion, who just ran behind the snapper. The snapper fakes it to him before snapping it way over to us. Cool, right?"

"So, anyway," Leach interrupts back, pulling on my arm again, "We called this guy's dad to ask if we could run that. We knew we could run it. Oregon had run it several years on an extra point. So, what we were calling about...?"

Pause. Awkward silence. Leach stares at the red carpet. Minshew points into the air to tell me to hang on. It's clear that he's been in this situation before. A lot. Suddenly, Leach re-fires.

"Yeah, we wanted to know who is still eligible to catch the ball on that play. I've got a wide receiver who is snapping it, and usually on that play that is the guy teams will immediately throw it back to, slipping into an open space after he snaps it. But this also means I have a center who is not really a center. So, can we turn that center into a receiver? Have him slip out there, too?"

Minshew cocks one eyebrow. "We used that formation in two games this year, against Wyoming and Oregon, but we never tried to throw it. Certainly not the center. We ran the ball."

Leach: "We didn't try to throw it to him because this guy's dad said we couldn't."

Finally, I get a word in: "Well, did it work when you ran the ball out of that formation?"

Minshew: "Every time. Maybe we should have tried to throw it to the center."

Leach, after another pause: "Maybe we still will. I haven't asked any Pac-12 officials what they think. But they might not be smart enough to know. I don't think there are any college presidents in that group."

CHAPTER 5

ACC-elerating

URING THE OFFSEASON between '82 and '83, Dad received a call from Mr. Neve. One of his veteran ACC field judges, Gerry Austin, was moving to the NFL. Dad was thrilled for Austin. He knew the pros was where Austin wanted to be, and now we know Austin's NFL tenure certainly backed that up, with a stack of Super Bowl appearances.

Neve asked Dad if he had enjoyed his brief time at back judge. Dad confessed that it had taken some adjustment to a new point of view, with the game coming directly at him, but yes, he liked it. Neve replied in his trademark terse tone, "Well, I was going to ask if you'd like to have Gerry Austin's spot at field judge, but if you like back judge that much, you can stay there."

Dad said, "Mr. Neve, you know what? Just this morning as I was driving to work, I was thinking to myself, 'Man, I sure would love to move to field judge.'"

Mr. Neve laughed aloud. That didn't happen a lot. It was like squeezing orange juice out of iron.

Dad

Of all the things I was fortunate enough to accomplish as an official, making Mr. Neve laugh might have been the greatest.

Dad worked a full ACC schedule in 1983. The crew was an All-Pro squad, including referee Courtney Mauzy, in his eighth year with the conference; back judge Doug Rhoads, an FBI agent who loved officiating so much he did it for free (the FBI didn't allow second paying jobs); Bud Elliott; Rex Stuart; and Don Robertson, who was in such ridiculously great physical condition he would officiate games on Saturday afternoons and enter marathons on Sunday mornings.

Dad

These guys were unflappable. They were also helpful. There was no jealousy with this group. Instead of holding the new guy at arm's length, they took me in and taught me. That's what the good guys do. That's what Mr. Gaddy and Mr. Clary had done. If you make me better, then that means I can make you better.

He and Mom talked about what that would mean on the home front. Once again, she pledged her support, but she also confessed some concern over the amount of autumn weekend nights Dad might be on the road. Even for the drivable Tobacco Road games, a Friday night stay was mandatory for any game that kicked off before 6:00 PM, which was most of them. The fly-in games meant at least one night, usually two. Dad pledged to be back home as soon as possible every

Sunday morning, and looking back, I don't think he ever missed church, even if it meant showing up in the middle of the sermon, having come straight from the airport.

A lot of those Sunday mornings, he found himself preached at, but not by the pastor. It was unsolicited feedback from the many fans of the Triangle area football teams, wanting to know why his crew had thrown that flag against North Carolina or didn't throw the flag on that obvious late penalty against Duke. They would even have complaints about calls that happened in all of the ACC games he hadn't worked.

Dad

People would be just adamant that I wasn't doing my duty as a true North Carolinian. "How in the world could you call that pass interference against the Tar Heels yesterday?! It cost them the game, Jerry...and you are *from here*!"

This went on for my entire career. In 1998, I had a game at North Carolina, and their All-American defensive back Dre Bly had intercepted a pass that set the ACC career interceptions record. The crowd went crazy and they made an announcement in the stadium; everyone was roaring. But I had a flag on the play. Defensive pass interference. If you know me, it has to be pretty egregious for me call it. My rule was that if I was going to throw my flag for a P.I. then I was going to have to throw it into a pool of blood.

I loved watching Dre Bly play football. But it was definitely a foul.

The next morning, I had a speaking engagement at a church in Charlotte. I was on Independence Boulevard, the busiest road in the city, and a big Cadillac pulled up next to me. The woman driving it saw me, did a double take, and rolled down her window. She had to be 90 years old and was dressed immaculately, obviously on her way to church.

She said, "Are you Dr. McGee, from the college?"

"Yes, ma'am, I am."

"You refereed the North Carolina game yesterday."

"Yes, ma'am, I did."

"Well, that call against Dre Bly SUCKED!"

And she rolled up her window and drove off.

Mom, Sam, and I learned to work around those Sunday morning conversations and complaints. We would field the early morning greetings of "Is your Dad going to make it to church today? I have a question for him about that ballgame..." and we would wait an few extra minutes to depart for post-church lunch at the Morrison's Cafeteria so that Dad could hold impromptu mini press conferences in the church vestibule and parking lot.

One morning, I was watching Dad explain a call to fellow parishioner and felt an arm around my shoulders. It was Ted Jackson, another Raleigh-based ACC official who attended our church. Today, he is one of the gurus of instant replay. Then, he was in the seventh season of his 28 as an on-field official. He said to me, "Everyone was mad at me last week, Ryan. You know what the preacher said to me? He quoted Jesus. 'Forgive, Ted, father. For he knows not what he does.'"

The most memorable example of such Sunday morning ire came during that first full ACC season of '83. It was Halloween weekend and the third-ranked Tar Heels were playing at No. 13 Maryland. With Clemson still on probation, it was a game that was going to determine the ACC championship as well as a New Year's Day bowl bid. There were representatives in attendance from the Orange, Sugar, Cotton, and Fiesta Bowls. The game was being broadcast on ABC, with Al Michaels and Lee Grosscup on the call, and with a late afternoon start it was guaranteed to end under the lights and in prime time.

It was a very big deal. It was also a very tight football game.

Quarterback Boomer Esiason led the Terrapins to a late score and two-point conversion to take a 28–17 lead late. But the Heels came back and with 22 seconds remaining UNC scored to trail 28–26. When they failed on the two-point conversion that would have tied the game, a very large percentage of the 51,200 fans at Byrd Stadium stormed the field and tore down the goal post in the enclosed west end zone, the very space of real estate where Carolina had just come up short.

But those 22 seconds were still on the clock and they had to be played. It took more than a half-hour to clear the field and restart the game. What happened next is still, more than three decades later, the play that Dad still finds himself forced to defend.

Dad

Everyone in America knew that Carolina was going to attempt an onside kick. Back then, that was a very aggressive, physical play. Today, the front line of the kicking team isn't allowed to run in there and start blocking the receiving team. In 1983 they could, like a flying wedge.

The kicker skulled the ball and then ran along behind it waiting for it to roll the 10 yards that it had to before he was allowed to pounce on it and recover it. His guys up front had cleared the path really well, and he scooped it up. But I had him just short of 10 yards. I mean, it was nine yards and two feet, but it was definitely short. I threw my beanbag to the turf to mark that spot, and I immediately looked across to Doug Rhoads on the other side of the field, and he had thrown his bean bag at that exact same spot. We both had the kicker touching it too soon, so it's Maryland's ball. One snap later, the game was over.

Once again, the fans flooded the field. This time, Dad and Doug Rhoads—a college administrator and an FBI agent—had devised an escape plan. During the long delay to get the first Maryland mob off the field, they'd decided that if a second wave came at game's end, they would sprint to the wall that lined the field and walk along against it, letting the crowd jump over them as they safely sneaked toward the locker room. It worked. Unfortunately, the other four members of the crew hadn't followed them.

Dad

Doug and I were sitting in the locker room, drinking water and talking about the game, and five minutes went by. Then ten minutes. Then fifteen minutes. We could hear helicopters and sirens, and we thought, "Damn, are they still playing?" Finally, the rest of the guys came in and they had lost their hats and their penalty flags, everything. They'd gotten caught up in the mob, and there were a handful of injured fans being airlifted out.

We had long talk there in the locker room about what we would have done had Carolina recovered that onside kick and had a chance to score in the end zone that now didn't have a goal post. We decided that if they'd gotten into field goal range, we would have flipped the field and moved them down to the end with a goal post.

That game actually caused a national rule change. From then on, until now, a stadium has to have a backup goal post ready to go in case that happens again.

Remember, this was my first real TV game during my first full-time season in the ACC. I was like, man, are they all going to be like this?

Oh yeah, speaking of TV, that's how we other three McGees were watching the game back in Raleigh. The images were dramatic. Al Michaels was even more dramatic. Especially when the grainy standard definition camera images of the onside kick captured under the dim lights of The Byrd were, well, just grainy and standard definition enough to create shadows of doubt in the court of public opinion, particularly those dressed in Carolina Blue. The difference between the ball rolling 10 yards and it rolling only nine yards and two feet was a little difficult to see on a 1980s 21-inch Zenith tube television.

Our phone started ringing. It didn't stop for quite a while. Mom was answering the calls from neighbors and family members, all of whom were Tar Heels loyalists. They were mad and they wanted to talk to Dad. They told her that there was already chatter on local radio that the game had been botched so badly by Dad and his crew that it would have to be replayed. She sent us to bed. Sam and I were a little stressed out.

Sam

I feel like over the years I, way more than Ryan, felt real stress during Dad's games.

Everyone else who is watching a football game, on TV or in the stands, they are rooting for one team or the other. My feelings were always that I didn't care who won. At a bowl game, I might buy a sweatshirt of one team and pull for them because I just thought they were a cool story, or I liked a certain player. But I just wanted was to see a great game and for Dad to have the chance to be a part of a great game. And I really wanted them to get it right.

That fear I'm talking about, what I never wanted was for the officiating crew to become the story. People would probably assume that as we got older, that stress level about that would come down. But as I grew up and understood the game at a higher level, I almost knew too much. You can't relax then, right?

Dad

When I would come home from a game, Hannah would say, "Great game. Ryan taped it for you." Ryan and I would go on runs together and we would talk about the game.

But Sam would come to me with a little sheet of paper, and it would have a handful of plays written down that he wanted to discuss, like: "3 minutes to go, 3rd quarter, 2nd and 8, pass interference..." I would say, "Okay, let's go get the tape and look at it."

The amazing thing was that the three or four plays Sam would have written down would always be the same three or four plays I was already thinking about, the ones I wanted to go back and review as soon as I got home. And he was in middle school!

Sam

I could get a little intense. If you know me, that's not a surprise. I can get a little intense now.

I always knew all the names of the officials and who was graded high and who was graded low, everything. So, when I would watch a game, whether Dad was on the crew or not, there was a pretty good chance that I knew that crew and everyone who was in it.

So, if I knew that the crew in the game I was watching was the best, and yet they still had a bad day and got some big calls wrong, my reaction was, "Geez, if these guys, the best, can foul up in the Rose Bowl or the Florida–Florida State game, then no official is immune to the nightmare game."

So, when Dad was on the field I was always thinking, *Let's not let this be the nightmare game for Dad, okay?*

Sam and I, ages 10 and 12, laid our heads down that night convinced that Dad had just had the nightmare game at Maryland. Mom never went to bed because she also believed her husband had just had the nightmare game. Meanwhile, Dad and referee Courtney Mauzy, both based in Raleigh, were laughing it up on their flight home, talking about Mauzy losing his hat and yellow flag as he fought his way through the celebrating Maryland crowd.

Dad

I got home at, like, two o'clock in the morning and every light in the house was on. Hannah was pacing the floor and all worked up. I asked her what was going on and she said, "They're talking about replaying the game because you guys screwed it up so bad!" I assured her that we hadn't screwed anything up and they damn sure weren't going to be replaying the game.

But then I thought, *Okay, maybe I should go check the tape before I go to bed. Just to be sure.*

At the start of the 1980s, there were still only a handful of college football games on TV each Saturday. But already Dad was starting to show up on TV quite a bit. My Dad! On TV!

It was such a big deal that we even took a family trip to an electronics trade show to purchase a new not-so-big-screen TV and our very first VCR. My job on Saturdays, starting perhaps that very night, was to make sure Dad's TV games were recorded. I would dutifully sit there with Mom and Sam, remote control in hand, pausing the recording during TV timeouts so that when Dad returned home, he could enjoy the luxury of commercial-free screening sessions. That remained my job throughout my teen years and even after I left for college, calling Mom from school to make sure she had the VCR timer set to roll tape on Pops, wherever he was.

As the years went on and I befriended other officials' families, I would quickly bond with my fellow audio-visual tech cohorts among each family. We shared horror stories of recording the wrong games and timers that were set too short and missed the ends of games. Then there was the worst tale of them all, when one ACC official rushed home from his first career bowl game, settled in with his beer and chips to take in his glorious performance...and the family had recorded over it with Robin Williams in *Popeye*.

Sam

It was real film study. As real as you could get watching a Jefferson-Pilot broadcast on a VHS tape. As much as he traveled, Dad never missed church. Sometimes he would meet us there straight from the airport and we'd eat lunch and go straight home and he would already have one or two plays in mind that he wanted to review. I watched how serious he was about it, and that's how I learned football. But it wasn't just watching a great play. It was watching how that play was covered by the officials on the field.

It was never just, "Man, look at how Keeta Covington from Maryland just outran everyone to the end zone on that punt return." It was, "Man, look at how the official adjusted in time and got back there to beat Keeta Covington to the end zone on that punt return."

Dad

I still have every game. Over the years, I collected this library of games that I would go back to all of the time. Those first days in the ACC, I had so many Maryland games with Bobby Ross. Over the next couple of decades, I had him again as the head coach at Georgia Tech and Army. Or Steve Spurrier, who was head coach at Duke and then went to Florida. Or Bill Dooley, who was at Virginia Tech and then Wake Forest. Or Lou Holtz at Notre Dame and then South Carolina. If I was going to see a coach or a team again, I would watch some old games of theirs to get ready. It couldn't hurt.

Plus, and I'm only sort of joking here, if one of those coaches still had a question about a call I had against them 10 years earlier, I could say, "It's funny you bring that up, Coach. I was just watching that play last Thursday..."

The Sunday morning after the UNC-Maryland onside kick, the church complainers were indeed lined up. How could Jerry—a *North Carolinian(!)*—have possibly believed that football hadn't rolled 10 yards?! Hadn't he heard Al Michaels and Lee Grosscup express their doubts?! And what the hell had they planned to do if Carolina had gotten to that end zone, trying to win the game without any goal posts?!

That Tuesday, Dad and Courtney Mauzy were both in attendance for a big Raleigh Chamber of Commerce luncheon. Everyone there was well aware of what the Meredith College VP and the hugely successful construction contractor did during their fall weekends, just as they were well aware of what game they had worked a few nights before. Dad asked Mauzy if anyone had spoken to him all day. "Nope." Dad replied, "Me, neither. Let's get out of here."

To the rest of the nation, that game has long been forgotten, even among Maryland fans. If they do remember it, they talk about the field storming and the goal post, not the onside kick. In fact, the story about the game that ran in *Sports Illustrated* the next week, titled CAROLINA'S COOKIE CRUMBLED AGAIN, never mentioned the onside kick.

But back home, because we are, you know, North Carolinians (!), the kick is what everyone remembers. A decade after the game, at a Baptist church conference, Mom was approached by an old friend she hadn't seen in years. When she tried to introduce her friend to Dad, the woman replied, "I don't have any interest in meeting your husband. He's the man who got the onside kick call wrong in that Carolina-Maryland game." Even now, as we were writing this book in 2020, I tweeted out a photo I found of Dad and the officiating crew at that game. The very first response was from an UNC alum and former employee: "Wait. Your dad was the FJ during the missing goal post and on-side kick fiasco?!"

Dad

By the way, here's the part no one remembers from that play. A flag had been thrown. Carolina was offsides on the kick. So even if it had gone 10 yards—which it still hasn't, by the way—they were going to have to kick it again.

And it so it was we learned early on that we would have to make room in our lives for confusion, misinformation, and unreasonably long stretches of anger from strangers and friends alike. That was all going to be a big part of this gig— and not just for Dad.

As Sam and I started attending games on a more regular basis, we developed a little bit of a comedy routine, though we were the only ones in on the joke. The comp tickets provided to the families of officials are typically in the cheap seats, located among the townies and those who love their team but who have never been in a campus classroom—only the campus bookstore. No matter what game it was or where, there would always be the one guy who believed the entire section was there to listen to him rag the refs. We would identify him early, and being the great fisherman that Sam McGee is, we'd let the guy run with the line in his mouth for a quarter or so, becoming braver and brasher with his comments to the men in stripes stationed below. Then, at precisely the right moment, I would stand and shout, "HEY! Stop picking on our dad!" Then Sam, a spot-on stand-in for the kid, Elliott, from the film *E.T.*, would drop his little head in puppy-dog sadness.

We'd hear nary a peep from that guy for the remainder of the game.

In case you hadn't already recognized a pattern when it came to those who were doing the shouting, complaining, and blaming, it has always been delivered 100 percent of the time from adults. At school, to our sports-loving friends who dressed head-to-toe daily in the colors of their favorite college teams, the McGee boys were looked upon as awesome.

Sam

Back then, you think about what TV coverage was, the only way that most people could consume college football was from a camera angle that was like you sitting in Row ZZ of the stadium. Well, our seats, bad as they might have been sometimes, a lot of times they were almost on the field. And then, at scrimmages and eventually games, we were on the sidelines! The only people who were getting closer to the game than us were the people who were actually playing in the game.

On one occasion, Sam got that close, too. Too close. It was during that same '83 season and it was a night that changed the direction of my life.

Sam

Dad was on the local news there in Raleigh after the UNC-Maryland game. They came to his office to ask him about that last play. Can you believe that? I remember he was totally confident about it as he explained it, but the Carolina fans still didn't want to hear it.

Then the reporter ended the interview by saying something like, "And hey, Carolina fans, you can see Jerry McGee in action again in another big game for the Tar Heels when they travel to Virginia in two weeks!"

In his second season at Virginia, George Welsh had the Cavaliers football program on the cusp of the turning the corner. UVA was 5–4 with two games remaining when the 19th-ranked Tar Heels came to Scott Stadium, another televised game as UNC was once again playing to impress the bowl scouts.

But the real story of that afternoon was that Dad and his crew had scored a sideline photographer's pass. It would be rotated per quarter between myself, Sam, and another official's kid. The previous Christmas, I had been gifted a brand-new, very fancy Sears-branded SLR camera and telephoto lens, delivered by Santa Claus himself. I had just completed a very successful football season as the yearbook photographer for the West Millbrook Middle School Wildcats. Now I was going to be snapping pics at Scott Stadium, standing alongside photographers from the *Richmond Times-Dispatch*, *Raleigh News & Observer*, and the *Washington Post*. They all looked at me with a perpetual WTH facial expression. But they also went way out of their way to help the just-turned-13-year old who stood among them, all 5-foot-5, 90 pounds of me.

The game was a tractor pull. UNC ran the ball behind the duo of Tyrone Anthony and Ethan Horton. Virginia was powered by a machine of a running back named Barry Word.

The contest ground into the fourth quarter, the scoreboard still struggling to climb into double digits. When that fourth quarter started, I would be back on the sideline with the coveted credential. But before that, it was Sam's turn.

Dad

We had a TV timeout and our crew was huddled up at midfield, trying to suck down some Gatorade and discuss what we'd seen so far before the teams came back out. We all agreed that this was getting pretty tense, and we talked about how it was a great crowd and a tight game. And then, I felt this tap on my leg…

I turned around and there is Sam. Right out in the middle of the field. The only people on the field were the crew of six officials and a 10-year old boy.

Sam says to me, "Hey, Dad. I just wanted you to know that I think you guys are doing a great job."

I look at Courtney Mauzy and he is as pale as his hat. I just put my arm around Sam and walked him back over the sideline. "Stay right here, okay? It'll be time to trade with Ryan again shortly."

Sam

Yeah…I don't remember that. And I usually remember everything. Maybe my brain has suppressed that memory because it knows I shouldn't have done it!

When the fourth quarter started, I re-commandeered the credential and took up a position right at the front pylon at the goal line on the end of Scott Stadium I knew Virginia would be driving toward. UVA was down 14–10 and in the closing minutes of the game were indeed marching toward the end zone where I stood. With time ticking down, Barry Word took a pitch to the short side of the field...*my* side of the field...avoided a couple of UNC tacklers and dove for the front corner pylon...*my* front corner pylon. I snapped the shutter on the camera. Word kept on coming. I somehow sidestepped him and he flew past me as he crashed into the ground. I remember looking down to see No. 11 hit the artificial turf at my feet with a thud.

Then, everything looked and sounded like it was going through a blender.

A UNC defender, too late to hit Word, instead hit me. Camera equipment and my ballcap and little plastic film canisters and, I think, my nylon Velcro wallet, containing a few bucks and a Jim Rice baseball card, it all went flying everywhere. The turf looked like a yard sale. You can't see the collision on TV. I've tried. I remember a couple of photographers leaning over to help me up, and they looked terrified. But I was not and popped right back up. The next morning my neck was a little sore, but in the moment I was running on pure adrenaline.

All I could think was, *This is the coolest job in the history of the world. When I grow up, I have to figure out a way to get paid to do this for a living.*

Up until that moment, what my father did on Saturday afternoons was always cool. But now, I understood how he felt about it on a whole new level. Everyone my age, we all still had years of sports remaining in our lives, so many games still ahead to put on a uniform and feel the energy that only comes with being on a field of play. For a teenager like me or a younger kid like Sam, we still had teams we would be members of, from middle school track and field to church league basketball to high school baseball. But for the overwhelming majority of us, reaching adulthood means also reaching the end of the line for competitive sports, being a part of a team, and the feelings that come with that. It's sad. It all goes away too fast.

But Dad got to keep going. He got to share the playing field with friends, coaches, athletes, and legends from among every one of those groups. In an instant, as if Barry Word had jarred something lose in my brain, I saw that. And from that day forward, I never once looked at what officials did the same way. They really loved it.

Dad

That same season, I took the whole family with me over to a game we were calling at Wake Forest. It was the first time we all went, all four of us. When the game was over, the families who had come to the game were waiting on us outside the locker room. It was great. But it was also really early in that first full ACC season, when we still trying to figure out how this was all going to work with Hannah and the boys and our lives at home that seemed to be getting busier every single day.

On the ride home that night, Hannah said to me, "I have never seen you look happier than I did when I saw you out there today in that game with your friends. I will never have any question as to why you do this."

It certainly wasn't for the money. In case you were wondering, the going rate for officiating a game and then coming home to have everyone at church mad at you, no one at the Raleigh Chamber of Commerce wanting to speak to you, and having your 13-year old son de-cleated by a future NFL linebacker was $200, plus $50 for travel. When Dad received his first ACC check in '82, he gave it to Mom. She used it to buy our first microwave.

A big part of the joy of the job for Dad was seeing new places, new players, and working with new officials from around the nation. In those days of six-man crews, a cross-conference matchup also meant a cross-conference lineup of officials. They called them split crews.

Dad

I loved working with split crews. Now, the traveling team brings officials from their conference, but back then we shared games. North Carolina used to play a big non-conference schedule. They played Auburn, Oklahoma, Kansas, so we'd work with guys from the SEC and Big 8. Maryland played what was an old-school Eastern football schedule. Outside of the ACC they had long rivalries with West Virginia, Syracuse, and Penn State. All of those teams were independent at the time, so they used a group of northeastern-based independent officials. They were really good. Years later, I worked with a lot of them after the formation of the Big East. Clemson played Georgia nearly every year, so we would split a crew with the SEC guys. Same when Georgia Tech would play Georgia and Auburn.

One weekend, Dad and backfield buddy Bill Booker traveled to Auburn for one of those ACC visits to The Plains.

This was the Pat Dye/Bo Jackson Era of Auburn football, a sleeping giant that had finally awakened and, in the years following the death of Bear Bryant, had become the state of Alabama's preeminent college football force. An excited Booker and McGee met their SEC coworkers at the hotel for their pregame meeting. But one of them was missing.

Dad

We are going over their SEC mechanics versus ours and they are giving us a heads-up on little things to watch for at Jordan–Hare Stadium. Finally, I said, "Hey, guys, I'd really feel a lot better about this if the back judge was here since we're going to be sharing a whole half of the field together. What's his name? Billy Teas?"

The SEC guys, they just kind of snickered and kept on with the meeting. Well, Billy Teas, he never showed up. We got dressed and went to the stadium, and still no Billy Teas. We're like an hour from kickoff. I'm thinking this is going to be a situation like those guys from Alabama who showed up at the last second for the game at Samford versus Guilford. But this is Auburn!

Booker and I decided to go walk the field. We get out there and there's a guy leaning up against the goal post, like Bear Bryant used to do. He was a little short guy with a big belly, smoking a cigarette. And he had on an official's uniform. I said to Booker, "Look at this damn guy. He put on a referee costume to get into the stadium for free."

The SEC guys walked out behind us, and the Auburn coaches are out there, and everyone's going, "Well, hey, Billy!" It was Billy Teas! And hey, man, Billy Teas, he ain't got time for meetings or getting the game balls, or any of that. Billy Teas, he only works when the game starts.

He called a nice game. Then, when it was over, the six of us got in the van to go back to the hotel, but not Billy Teas. I never saw him again.

Aside from the occasional back judge skipping the pregame to burn a pack of Marlboro Reds, the age of the split crews was a model of cooperation and learning fresh takes on the football officiating craft. No matter what conference or region the crews came from, nearly 100 percent worked hard, worked together, and officiated every play of every game in the fairest manner possible.

Note: that's *nearly* 100 percent.

In the days before this current era of Power 5 super conferences, the eastern half of the college football map was covered with independent schools, really good programs with no conference affiliation. In the north, the independents included Notre Dame, Penn State, Syracuse, Pittsburgh, West Virginia, and Boston College. In the south, the list included the likes of Miami, Florida State, Virginia Tech, and South Carolina, which had bolted from the ACC in 1971, citing the unfair politics and power of the Tobacco Road basketball schools.

Those regional groups of independents also had their own rosters of football officials. The overwhelming majority of those officials operated on the up-and-up. When conference realignment re-sorted the college football landscape at the end of the decade, those former independent officials went on to have great careers in the ACC, SEC, Big East, and elsewhere. Some of the biggest games Dad ever worked were alongside officials who came from those independent ranks, and they remain his great friends to this day.

But scattered among that long list of great officials and people were a couple of bad ones.

When Dad speaks of the moment that he realized that there were conspirators in his midst, his tone is that of a man who still can't believe what he knows to have been true.

Dad

Clemson–South Carolina is a vicious rivalry. I worked that game five times. The first time, I was scheduled for Duke–North Carolina, but the ACC supervisor called and said they needed me down at Clemson. It was a split crew with some of the independent guys. He said, "I need you there because I think we've got real problems in this game. They've got one guy on that crew who has a questionable reputation, and they have another guy in there who we all know cheats."

That game always has the most intense atmosphere anyway, but as soon as we hit the field, there's Danny Ford, all lathered up before we've even kicked off. He was pointing across the field at one of the guys in particular. "Everyone in this stadium knows that S.O.B. cheats! Y'all don't let him screw us!"

Now, never in 400 games did I even once time think that a coach was trying to get me to make a call to help him. But coaches are, by nature, paranoid about somebody screwing them. Danny Ford wasn't saying to me, "I want you to look after me." What he was saying, knowing that we already had our concerns, was, "Don't let him be the guy that takes this game from us."

Around that same time, very early in Dad's career, a coach had summed it up when he spoke of split crews: "I think all referees are sumbitches. But at least with the ACC guys I know they're our sumbitches."

Dad

Here I am at one of the biggest games I've worked and I just can't believe this is even happening, you know? But the way the system was set up then, I suppose there was always going to be someone, even if was just one or two guys, who were going to try and pull something over.

The system he is referring to how bowl assignments used to be determined for college football officials. Back then, there were only 18 postseason bowl games. The number of officiating crews from each conference who received a postseason invitation was based on the number of schools from that conference that made it into those bowl games, a half-crew per team.

For example, in 1984, the Big Ten had five teams earn bowl bids. That meant that the Big Ten had also earned the honor of sending two and half of its officiating crews to bowl games—15 men total—to some combination of the 13 postseason games that didn't have a Big Ten team on the field.

These two independent officials standing across the field from Dad that night at Clemson had become notorious for trying to help their teams win games late in the season, when they were within a striking distance of a win total that would earn them a postseason bowl bid, and in turn possibly them, too. A win over Clemson would earn the Gamecocks a New Years' Day bowl. They won by one point.

Dad is confident that his two questionable crewmates failed to determine the outcome of the game, but it wasn't for lack of trying. The following night, Dad and his ACC cohorts from the game received a call from the league office. Had they seen anything fishy? Yes, they said, they had. The two suspects had tried to cheat a yard here or there on multiple spots and there was at least one phantom foul on a big play.

There were no makeup calls made by the four good guys. That would be as dishonest as the original crimes. There were disagreements and "moving spots" were corrected by the other members of the crew when they needed to be fixed.

Dad

What drove you crazy was you had to work a game with these questionable guys, and then the holidays come along and two good officials are sitting at home, watching the Cotton Bowl or the Sugar Bowl, and there are those jerks on the field.

The very next season I had Miami and Maryland at Memorial Stadium in Baltimore. The defending national champions versus another top 20 team. Split crew. Another game with a couple of guys we didn't trust. We're sitting in the Orioles dugout. That was our locker room there. One of them says to me, "Jerry, what's the penalty for an offensive facemask?" I told him it was 15 yards, but I also said I didn't know if I'd ever even seen one called before, at any level. Sure enough, Maryland had a long offensive play, and boom, offensive facemask. We're live on CBS, a one-score game, and we're looking at him like, *Are you serious?!*

All you could do was fix everything you could catch as it happened during the game and let those guys know you knew what was happening and you weren't putting up with it.

Only once did it boil over into a real fight. It was at half-time of another Clemson–South Carolina game. A touch-down had been called back, and the umpire, an ACC guy, was waiting in the locker room, shouting, "You are going to let the kids on the field decide this game!" The two officials had to be separated.

Dad

I was thinking, how are we going to call the second half if we were missing two officials?

In the end, you report it to your supervisor and hope maybe someone will do something about it. Back then, it was more of the Wild Wild West when it came to how officiating was governed. Today, that wouldn't even last a game.

Once realignment took place, the era of the independents ended and the governance of officiating fell under a much more deliberate set of national checks and balances. It also helped when television became widespread and there was nowhere for the small handful of cheaters in stripes to hide. And once the men who'd had to share the field with those rules-benders moved into the roles of league and national officiating supervisors, the game's small handful of shady characters went the way of the leather helmet. Split crews also went away, to the chagrin of many officials who enjoyed working with out-of-conference colleagues, and the visiting conference began providing the crews for cross-conference games. The archaic "bowl bids equals bowl assignments" model was also scrapped. Today, the 40-plus bowl games are distributed evenly between the Power 5 (five bowls each) and Group of

5 (three each) conference officiating groups, as assigned by the national college football officiating coordinator.

The coincidental twist in all of this is that at season's end, Dad received his first bowl assignment, and it was also South Carolina's bowl assignment. The No. 7 Gamecocks took on No. 9 Oklahoma State and running back Thurman Thomas in the 1984 Gator Bowl.

His next game was even bigger, the season opener at Maryland, ranked preseason No. 1 by *Sport Magazine*, but which lost to a Penn State team that would play in the next national title game. For Dad, the year ended with his second bowl game, a showdown between the '84 national champs, BYU, and Ohio State.

Sam

We didn't go to Dad's first bowl game, but we went to the second one. It was the Citrus Bowl, and we did it all. We went to Disney World. I remember it was awesome because you had all of these fans from all of the Florida New Year's bowl games at Disney World, cheering and giving each other a hard time.

We went to Kennedy Space Center. The Challenger was actually on the launch pad, a month before the explosion. Ryan had just been to Space Camp, so that was a really big deal, and after the accident, we watched that explosion over and over again, trying to figure out what happened. It was the second-most watched piece of video ever recorded at our house.

The most-watched was recorded at nearly the same time. Dad had a touchdown call in that game. Robbie Bosco, the BYU quarterback, had scrambled to the far side of the field, and then he threw back across the field, nearly all the way to the other sideline, like a 40-yard bomb. It was a totally busted play, so the receiver had come back into the middle of the field, caught it, and then turned and kind of dived toward the front pylon with the defender right behind him.

The way the mechanics were then, Dad was so tight up on the players all the time and the play had moved so far to other side of the field, the receiver and the defensive back got behind him, between him and goal line. That would never happen now.

So, Dad was running up the sideline behind the receiver when he was headed for the pylon, the defender was between them. He got into the end zone, but there was some question about whether or not his foot had stepped out of bounds before the ball broke the plane.

It happened all at once. Dad signaled touchdown. But he was convinced he'd missed it.

I don't know if anyone has ever driven from Orlando to Raleigh faster than we did after the game. As soon as we hit the door of our house, we were rewinding the tape on that play. We watched it a hundred times. This is 1985. There's no goal line camera or pylon cam. Just two angles, both blurry on the replay.

The whole time, Dad is saying, "I think he stepped out of bounds." And the whole time, I'm saying, "Nope. You got it right. Touchdown."

We still don't agree on it.

I sincerely hope that every family has a stretch in their lives together like we had in the 1980s. I remember it as pure joy, and football was such a huge part of that.

Sam and I continued to get sideline credentials and I continued to take photos. It was at Duke's Wallace Wade Stadium, the place where Pa-Pa had taken Dad to his first college football game, that I first experienced the magic of the press box. At halftime, the local photographers said, "Come with us, kid," and we marched up through the grandstand like royalty. We arrived to the press box and they gave us boxed lunches that included a hot dog *and* a pulled pork sandwich, with a bag of potato chips, a giant chocolate chip cookie, and all the Pepsi a kid could drink. As we sat around tables eating, Mike Krzyzewski walked by, coming off his first winning season next door at Cameron Indoor Stadium, and said hello to the table. So did Miss North Carolina. Then we descended back to the field for the second half.

Sam

It became such a regular part of our lives that my friends had to remind me how crazy it all really was. I remember one of my best friends in middle school saying to me, "So, you're going to the game at UNC this weekend, you were at the game at Virginia last weekend, and you were the ball boy at an NC State practice yesterday? You realize this isn't normal, right?"

But for us, it was.

Those friends were all-in. The two most exciting moments of the season for college football officials and their families were the delivery of the fall schedule, which back then arrived via the late summer mail, and the news of whether or not that season would end with a trip to a bowl game, a phone call that came the week after the regular season had ended and the bowl invitations to teams had become official. I still remember the pride that swelled in my chest when I was sitting in Mr. Gaines' 12th grade Western Civilizations class at Travelers

Rest High School and a student office assistant appeared in the doorway with a phone message for me. I went to the door and the note simply read, WE'RE GOING TO THE GATOR BOWL! MICHIGAN STATE VS. GEORGIA. I announced it to the class, amid much applause and high fives as I returned to my seat.

Dad always wore a sweatband on his left wrist, underneath a black digital watch that he used to keep the on-field clock. It was practical, yes. But it was also a fantastic visual cue that separated him from the other officials on the crew. To this day, when a game pops up on ESPN Classic or YouTube, Sam and I spot Dad immediately, thanks to that black-and-white left wrist. Our classmates and friends also picked up on that Dr. McGee trademark, for better or worse, when he was officiating a game involving their favorite team. They would also mimic his very distinct lean-forward running style. In college, my dorm roommates would take to the intramural fields running in a line, all leaned forward doing their best Dr. McGee impersonation.

Sam

One Saturday, those same college friends of Ryan's were all in town with him and we headed down to Death Valley for Duke at Clemson. We had Pa-Pa with us.

Keep in mind, this is the same Pa-Pa who was in attendance for Dad's first game at Clemson a year earlier and the same man who took little Jerry McGee to his first college football game at Duke...because Marshall Caddell was a proud Methodist and thusly a Duke Blue Devils fan.

Sam

We didn't have the usual bad free officials' tickets. We had skybox seats from a food service company that Dad worked with at his day job. This was really before you saw skyboxes anywhere, but Death Valley had them before everyone else, of course. The game started and I asked Pa-Pa who he was rooting for, and he said, "Well, these Clemson people are taking really good care of us. So, I think it's only right to root for Clemson."

But halfway through the game, Duke was hanging in there. Pa-Pa had been chatting everyone up, but now he was getting kind of quiet. I said, "You still rooting for Clemson?"

Pa-Pa shook his head no. He was done denying his Duke roots. He said to me, "It's a sad frog who can't pull for his own pond."

Pa-Pa and my friends alike would start calling the house every summer, asking, "Your Dad get his schedule yet?" We'd spend those summers watching him studying his rulebook by the neighborhood swimming pool, and by mid-June he would always start getting twitchy. "Man, the schedules should be coming out soon, right?" When his game assignments finally did arrive, typically the entire year all at once, it was all about scanning that list for big games and new locations.

I can distinctly remember the excitement that came in '87 when UNC at Oklahoma was on the list.

Dad

When coaches would fill out their postgame evaluations, they would give you a grade from 0 to 10. And, big surprise, the losing coach would often give you a zero and the winning coach would give you a 10.

But the best part of those evaluation forms was that there was a comments section at the bottom. We worked that Carolina–Oklahoma game and UNC was pretty bad, but Oklahoma was a machine. They were No. 1 in the country and they had Keith Jackson and Ricky Dixon and Jamelle Holieway at quarterback. They won that game 28–0.

The evaluation comes in from Barry Switzer, head coach at Oklahoma. He gave us great grades. But then he wrote at the bottom: "Don't ever send Booker and McGee back out here. Next time send Billy the Kid and Jesse James, because at least I know they're going to rob me."

Where there were open weekends in Dad's ACC schedule, he would quickly fill them with dates at smaller schools, in one part to keep busy, but also to help mentor young officiating talent at the lower levels, just as had been done for him not too long ago. The most frequent destination was Statesboro, Georgia, home of Georgia Southern University. The Eagles were the Oklahoma Sooners of I-AA football, a wishbone-powered running machine that reached the national championship game four times in five years and won three titles.

Their head coach was Erk Russell, arguably the most famous defensive assistant coach in college football history as the mastermind behind Georgia's "Junkyard Dawg" defense. Russell was known for head-butting players, smashing his exposed bald dome against their helmets until there was blood trickling down his forehead. He held so much sway over UGA that he even worked with the marching band to come up with a playlist to get the crowd fired up, injecting Jim Croce's "Bad,

Bad Leroy Brown" between the hedges whenever the Dawgs
got a big stop.

Erk Russell was a character. He also worked very hard to
find any advantage he could on the field.

Dad

We were in the locker room there at Georgia Southern,
having our pregame meeting. It was a little place and had
one bathroom right off the main room. When we'd get to the
stadium, they would just give us a key to that locker room
and tell us to make sure to give it back before we left that
evening. We're having our meeting and we're talking about
the tendencies of the teams and what we needed to keep an
eye on. It was the first game of the year, so we were also discussing new rules changes, how they might affect the game
early on. That kind of thing.

We start wrapping up the meeting and all of the sudden
the bathroom door opens. Erk Russell comes walking out. He
acted all surprised to see us, "Oh, hey, sorry, guys, I didn't
know you'd already be in here. Just needed to go to the bathroom and I needed some privacy. Have a great game." Well,
hell, he'd obviously been in there listening to our meeting.

I was back down there at the very end of the season. We sat
down to have our meeting, and I realized that Coach Russell
was in there again. So, I said, "You know what, guys? Let's
head outside and take a look at the field..." and when we left,
I locked the door.

We started getting close to kickoff, and you could feel
everyone asking, "Have you seen Coach Russell?" Finally, we
went back to the locker room for one last pit stop before the
game started. When I unlocked the door, Erk Russell came

flying out of there and headed straight for the field. "Oh, hey, sorry, Coach. We didn't know you were in there!"

I came back to Georgia Southern one more time before he retired in 1989. He was not hiding in the bathroom this time.

We had also moved again, right into the heart of the same legendary league packed with Georgia Southern's biggest rivals. Dad was now vice president of development at Furman University, member of the Southern Conference, the grandparent conference of the SEC where the Paladins battled the likes of Marshall University, Western Carolina, and Appalachian State. No sooner had we moved to Greenville, South Carolina, than I found my way into the press box, keeping statistics for the Furman Paladin Radio Network. And while Dad was on the sidelines at Louisville ("Howard Schnellenberger really liked to haze young officials") and Florida State ("Burt Reynolds was a really nice guy"), Sam was working the sidelines of Paladin Stadium as a ball boy.

Sam

I took that very seriously. In my mind, I was just like Dad. I had to get my mechanics down perfectly. Keep in mind, one of Dad's duties was always to get game balls on and off the field, so now I was on the other side of that, and I knew just how important my job was. When did you know Dad was really on top of a game? When a guy would break a long touchdown run and Dad would still beat him to the goal line. Anticipate the play and stay ahead of it. That was my approach, too. I was never prouder than when a long play would happen and the field judge would be way downfield, had just signaled, and he would look way back up the field for a new football, but instead he would find me standing right beside him.

That might sound a little obsessive to some people, but man, I was doing my part.

Sam also developed Dad's thick skin when it came to being screamed at. The Furman coaching staff was packed with staffers who also went on to win rings at schools throughout college football. Bobby Johnson, the future head coach at Vanderbilt, has always been revered as a gentleman of the game. But let's just say he wasn't very gentle on the ball boys at Furman.

The Paladins won the 1988 NCAA I-AA national championship, defeating Georgia Southern. Unfortunately, the game was played in Pocatello, Idaho, so only Dad was able to make the trip. But it was a thrill to watch the game on ESPN that night. And it was an even bigger thrill when Doug Holliday, the radio voice of the Paladins, thanked me over the air for my stats work during the regular season. Years later, Dad even gave me his national championship ring, engraved with MCGEE VP on the side.

Sam

I think it's time to finally get this off my chest. I should have that ring. I was on the field that year.

It's a fair point. But that doesn't mean I'm giving it to him. Besides, he should have won his own the following season, when Furman was once again marching through the NCAA playoffs and hosted Stephen F. Austin in the national semifinals. There was a rare Upstate South Carolina blizzard that day, so Sam and the ball boys were working extra hard. So were the I-AA officials assigned to the game—though as they learned at game's end, perhaps not hard enough. The 15-year old ball boy with the extensive knowledge of the rulebook made sure of that, especially when it came to onside kicks.

Sam

This is in the closing seconds of the game. Furman had just scored and trailed 21-19. We had a great long placekicker on that team, so if Furman gets the ball back and completes just one pass, this guy, Glen Connally, is more than likely going to make the game-winner and determine who is moving on to play for the national championship.

Everyone sets up for the onside kick and I see that the field judge isn't lined up 10 yards downfield from the kicker. With the snow he was confused and had lined up at 15 yards instead. So, I'm going to help this guy out. I ran over to the correct spot and said to him, "I'm standing at 10 yards! I'm standing at 10 yards!" The ball is kicked and Furman recovers and they say, nope, it didn't go far enough, Stephen F. Austin's ball.

Now I am standing at the spot where the ball was recovered and I am saying to the guy, "It went 12 yards! This is 12 yards right here!" And he actually engaged me. He looked at me and said, "No, no, it was only eight yards, this is the line." Now I'm just screaming, "No! No! THIS is the line! Look, we can step it off from where he kicked it. I'm at the 45, you're at midfield."

In a complete role reversal, Dad was there as a spectator, his regular season over, and was watching Sam down on the field.

Dad

It was obvious that the crew was confused because they huddled on the field to discuss it. We were in the press box with my boss, the Furman president, and I had just told him that I didn't think this was going to go our way. Then I looked over on the sideline and there was someone jumping up and down and pointing down to the correct spot. It was Sam.

Sam

The game ended, and I actually followed the white hat off the field. "The ball went 10 yards!" He looked at me like I had two heads. *Who the hell is this 15-year old? Wasn't he a ball boy?* And they ran in the locker room. Season over.

Dad

We were watching the officials leave and I thought, *Oh damn, Sam is following them off the field!* I looked over at Hannah and she was watching him, too. She just looked at me like, "Well, there goes our boy."

One week later, Stephen F. Austin lost 37–34 in the national title game at Georgia Southern, after which Erk Russell retired from coaching. No word on whether or not he was hiding in the officials' locker room toilet during the pregame.

Coach's Timeout
with Vince Dooley

"I would say that there was about a 98 percent chance that Erk was eavesdropping on your father's crew down in Statesboro."

It is 12:30 PM on December 7, 2019, in Atlanta's World Congress Center, and I am sitting onstage alongside Vince Dooley, former longtime Georgia head coach, athletic director, and boss to Erk Russell. Coach Dooley is about to be a guest on *Marty & McGee*, the show I am fortunate enough to cohost with my friend Marty Smith on ESPN Radio and the SEC Network. In a few hours, Dooley's former team will be on the field next door at Mercedes-Benz Stadium, playing LSU in the SEC Championship Game. But right now, we are making small talk until the production truck says they are rolling.

"Your father officiated my last game as head coach, did he not?"

He did. It was that 1989 Gator Bowl contest against Michigan State, the one I had made such a proud presentation about in Western Civ class.

"I let my successor, Ray Goff, call that game however he wanted, and we were throwing it all over the place, and so was Michigan State. We made Andre Rison a millionaire in that game," he said of the Spartans wide receiver who caught nine passes for 252 yards and a trio of touchdowns. Four months later, Rison was taken in the first round of the NFL draft. "We had a touchdown lead late in that game and I remember telling the official on my sideline, 'I can't take this throwing it. I'm a nervous wreck! This is my last few minutes on the job, so we are going to run the ball!' and we did. Was that your father I was talking to?"

I told him no. Dad was across the field that night, on the Michigan State sideline chatting with the other head coach, George Perles. Dooley was likely talking to Dr. Bud Robertson, who was also in his last game, closing out a distinguished 16-year officiating career in the ACC.

"That's right!" the coach exclaimed. "You know, Bud and I became great friends. I reached out to him when I was doing some Civil War research. Only then did I realize he had been a football official."

Dr. James I. "Bud" Robertson was perhaps the foremost historian on that war, ever. Robertson was the author of more than 40 books, including the seminal biography of Stonewall Jackson. He was a professor at Virginia Tech for 44 years, teaching more than 25,000 students, where he would see Vince's brother, Virginia Tech head coach Bill Dooley, on campus. In the 1970s, he'd officiated Bill Dooley's games when he was head coach at UNC. In 1987–88, he officiated Dooley's games at Wake Forest. "Dr. Bud" held three college degrees, earned professor emeritus status and was considered for the Pulitzer Prize. In 1961, he was appointed by John F. Kennedy as executive director of the United States Civil War Centennial Commission. He was only 30 years old.

Vince Dooley became emotional as he spoke, because Dr. Robertson had passed away just that week. I made him laugh by telling him about the night before the Gator Bowl, New Year's Eve, when the officiating families walked Jacksonville Riverwalk together and Dr. Bud the academician wore a self-made crown of neon Glo-sticks bought from a street vendor, his face totally deadpan.

Vince Dooley laughed and asked who else was on that crew. I told him it was Dad, the soon-to-be university president; Mauzy, the self-made millionaire; Bill Booker, the lifelong high school teacher and coach; attorney and former Clemson lineman Clark Gaston; construction mogul Bill Jamerson; and financial advisor Billy Lovett, once Maryland football's all-time leading rusher, who went on to officiate a Super Bowl.

"Wow. Such an impressive, impressive group of men. But you know what?" Dooley said as our interview had ended and he grabbed my hand for a goodbye shake. "There were about 80,000 people there at my last game that night, and they were all completely convinced that those seven guys were the biggest idiots in the building."

Then the College Football Hall of Famer winked at me.

"Unless we had blown that lead. Then they would have all been ranked behind me."

CHAPTER 6

THE WALL
OF SCREAMING

VINCE DOOLEY WASN'T TYPICALLY a sideline screamer. The reality is that during Dad's four decades of sideline experience, very few of the coaches were the kind of guys who spent entire games ranting and hollering about everything that happened.

> **Dad**
>
> It was usually the complete opposite of that, especially when you were working with coaches and staff members you had seen over and over again for years. A lot of times, they would give me a heads-up on what was coming, maybe even just a whisper before a play, "Hey McGee, we are about to throw this pass directly at the spot where you are standing, you might want to take a couple of steps back."
>
> One day at Georgia Tech, a team that ran the ball on every single play, one of the offensive coaches casually walked over and said, "Be on your horse for the first three plays. We are going to throw the living hell out of it." They did it, too, like three straight bombs downfield, and I was ready for it. I was

in perfect position on every play. In the postgame, the evaluator was Dan Post, a guy I'd officiated with for years. He says, "God almighty, you were on top of all those early pass plays. You beat the receiver downfield on every one of them! Did you know that was coming?"

I said, "I don't know, man. I guess I'm just that fast."

But all of that being said. Even the good guys have bad days.

As Dad tells that story, we are in his home in Charlotte, North Carolina. These days he lives only a few miles away from me, and Sam lives at almost the precise halfway point between us. It's the first time since those days in the 1980s that we have all lived in the same place.

He is talking about interacting with coaches on the sideline and how he always worked hard to adhere to another of Mr. Norval Neve's oft-repeated commandments of officiating advice.

Dad

He would say, "You will get in more trouble for what you say on the sideline than what you call in the game."

I would be lying if I said I always stuck to that rule. But I certainly always tried to.

There are two rooms here in Dad's house that are decorated almost exclusively in sports memorabilia. One is his personal collection of baseball stuff. I call it McCooperstown. The other is the TV room, where he now spends many of his college football Saturdays, watching games between four walls that are covered in mementos from his own days on the field. In the houses of my youth, his walls were covered with the pennants of the nearly 150 different teams he shared the field with. His current collection is more modest, though that's a relative term.

There are so many commemorative coins, flipped before so many games gone by. There is a stack of program covers from those games. Dad used to have those covers photographed and put into framed collages depicting each season's schedule, but he quit doing that after a while because "when you start something like that, you don't expect to do it for 30 years."

There are ring and watch display boxes packed with jewelry engraved with the logos of games ranging from the Plymouth Holiday Bowl and Sega Las Vegas Bowl to the classic red Rose Bowl emblem, set in gold. Wherever Dad wears it, it's a showstopper.

But the space that always grabs the attention of visitors is what I have always called the Wall of Screaming. It's a series of framed photos purchased from newspaper photographers around the nation, images we spotted on Sunday mornings at airport newsstands while waiting to fly back from games, or, in later years, on university websites. Many of them are big moments. Standing at the goal line as Penn State's Curtis Enis hauls in a touchdown against USC in the Kickoff Classic at the Meadowlands in '96. Laughing it up with Frank Howard at Clemson in '86. Standing with the Florida State captains moments before marching to midfield for the coin toss at the inaugural ACC Championship Game in '05. Eyeballing a diving catch by Georgia Tech's James Johnson vs. archrival Georgia in the game they call "Clean, Old-Fashioned Hate."

However, the best photos are of the angry coaches.

There's Joe Morrison, the man who built South Carolina into something other than an also-ran, who introduced the

Gamecocks' black jerseys and their *2001: A Space Odyssey* stadium entrance, on the sideline during the Clemson game of '84. "Old Dependable" is screaming, his jaw unhinged, and appears to be pointing directly at Dad, who appears to be totally ignoring the coach.

The caption that accompanied that photo in the Sunday morning paper read: COACH JOE MORRISON EXPLAINS HIS POINT OF VIEW TO A LESS THAN INTERESTED OFFICIAL.

Dad

I don't think he's even actually yelling at me, but the camera angle sure makes it look like he is, doesn't it? I don't know. Maybe he was. What I do remember about that game was that I had to get the South Carolina captains for the coin toss, but no one knew who the captains were because Morrison picked them game-by-game. They told me I needed to ask him, and they walked me down to a door under the stadium. I opened it, and there was Joe Morrison, sitting totally alone on a folding chair in the middle of an empty concrete room. There was one light bulb hanging right over him, like a spotlight, and the room was full of smoke. He was sitting there, basically in the dark, chain smoking like crazy before the game.

"Uh...Coach, I need to know who your captains are..."

There's Lou Holtz, coaching in that same game 15 years later, finishing up his first year at South Carolina with an 0–11 record and a 31–21 loss to Clemson. In this photo, Dad is walking toward Holtz, likely delivering yet another dose of bad news at the end of a season full of it. The coach has his arms folded and his face buried in one hand.

Dad

South Carolina was actually in that game way longer than anyone expected them to be. I hadn't seen Lou in a few years, and when he spotted me during the pregame, he laughed said, "Jerry, I'm 0–10 and I need a friend so badly I'm going to hug an official."

Several years ago, I showed a copy of the photo to Holtz. He said, "I wasn't mad at your father at that moment. I am pretty sure what I was thinking was, 'Now, where exactly am I going to take my wife, Beth, on vacation once this season is finally over?'"

The most notable photo on the Wall of Screaming was taken in Tuscaloosa, Alabama, on October 6, 2006, when Duke visited Alabama. Crimson Tide head coach Mike Shula is standing, at most, two feet off the back of Dad's head, his mouth wide open and his hand extended to underline the point he's so angrily exclaiming. Once again, Dad seems to be purposely ignoring it, looking toward the scoreboard clock as he fills out his penalty card with the details of the foul that Shula is so unhappy about.

Alabama won that game 30–14, the third-from-last win of Shula's four-year Tuscaloosa tenure. Six weeks later, he was fired. They replaced him with some guy named Nick Saban.

Dad

When I look at that picture, what I think about is the amount of pressure these coaches are under. When Mike Shula was unloading on me that night, he probably already knew he was finished. It's a reminder that you never truly know what's going on with a coach behind closed doors.

The reality is that over 404 games of college football officiating, almost all of it on the sideline, I only remember a very few times when a coach truly just flipped out on me. And looking back, like Shula that night, there was almost always something else behind it.

Take, for instance, Jim Young. During Young's 17 years as head coach at Arizona, Purdue, and Army, he was universally considered one of the truly good guys of college football. So, Dad was shocked on September 27, 1986, when Wake Forest traveled to West Point and his experience on Young's sideline at Michie Stadium was a cacophony of cuss words. The Black Knights were favored in the game by a couple of touchdowns, but instead were trailing the Demon Deacons early en route to a blowout upset loss.

There was a bad call late in the second quarter, a defensive pass interference flag on the other side of the field. Those officials were too far away to hear Young, so he aimed his anger at the field judge, the ref who was most easily at his disposal. He stalked Dad up and down the sideline, screaming over and over again, "You have already f--ked up this entire game!"

Sam

I think football fans assume an official is out there just looking for a reason to throw his penalty flag, but the good ones have the complete opposite approach. Typically, if a player draws an unsportsmanlike penalty, or even something like a holding, there's a really good chance the official has already warned them about it at least once. *Keep that up, and we're going to have to flag you.*

Anyone who doesn't believe that needs to do what we have always done, and really watch how a good sideline official reacts to a coach who has spent a ridiculous amount of time in the game screaming, yelling, and complaining. The official will walk away from a coach like that. They will warn him directly. They will even go to other people on the sideline and say, "Hey, someone needs to calm him down before he draws an unsportsmanlike." If it keeps it up after that, there is going to be a penalty. Or, if he breaks the golden rule.

Ah yes, the golden rule. When it comes to flagging a coach with a personal foul, the guideline is very simple. You only unfurl the yellow napkin when their rants have become personal. For example: "That's was the stupidest goddamn call I've ever seen!" is okay. But "You are stupidest goddamn human being I have ever seen!" is not. If you need a more detailed illustration, please watch the film *Bull Durham* and the scene where Crash Davis calls the umpire the one name he knows you can never call an umpire, because he's trying to get thrown out of the game and perhaps get his teammates to finally become fired-up and focused.

Jim Young kept railing, and it was getting worse. Dad went to the Army assistant coaches and asked them to tell their boss to cool off, because he didn't want to flag the supposed nicest man in football. They told Dad no way, he was on his own.

Dad

The clock is ticking down to the end of the first half, and he is just getting louder and louder. I'm watching the clock thinking, *Okay, we're going to be saved by the bell here.* Then, with about 38 seconds remaining, Young leaned right into my ear and screamed, "You guys are just a bunch of goddamn sonsofbitches, aren't you?!" I threw my flag. Personal foul, 15 yards.

I went in to the white hat, Bob Cooper, and he said, "What in the hell have you done? That's probably the nicest head coach in America."

I said, "Well, I flagged him."

Bob said, "Why? What did he say?"

"He called me a goddamn sonofabitch."

Bob said, "Well, you are a goddamn sonofabitch."

I told Bob, "Well, he said you were a goddamn sonofa-bitch, too."

Bob said, "Well, then give me that damn football…" and he marked off the 15-yard penalty.

Nearly a decade later, Dad was back at Michie Stadium for a Rutgers-Army matchup, as part of a Big East officiating crew. As that crew held their pregame meeting, in walked Jim Young, now retired as a football coach but still omnipresent in West Point as a living legend. Young introduced himself to the room.

Dad

When I said my name, he said, "You know, there used to be a McGee who officiated in the ACC." I told him, yeah, I know. It was me. He said, "You are the only official who ever flagged me during a game."

I asked him, "Well, did you deserve it?" And Coach Young said, "Oh, hell yes; the only mistake you made was that you didn't flag me five minutes earlier. Sorry about that, I was just trying to do something to wake my team up."

Just like Crash Davis.

One night at Virginia, George Welch started riding Dr. Earnest Benson, a veteran ACC official who was also a longtime educator at Albany State. Welch wouldn't stop. He, too, had gotten personal, saying something about Dr. Benson's relationship with his mother. So, Benson threw his flag: unsportsmanlike conduct, Virginia.

When the crew gathered midfield to discuss the penalty, someone asked, "Ernie, where's your flag?" When they all turned back toward the sideline to see if it was on the turf, they spotted Welch, who was still stomping up and down that sideline...unaware that Dr. Benson's yellow penalty flag was sitting on his shoulder.

Dad

Another night at Virginia, Booker had a pass interference penalty against UVA during what was already a really bad night. A few minutes later, there was a TV timeout and I walked by Booker there on the Virginia sideline. He said, "Did I get that call right?" I told him, "Yes, it was a great guess." So, he smiled at me, tobacco sticking all out of his teeth and said, "Well, kiss me."

I just lost it laughing, right there on the field.

The next week we got our evaluation from Coach Welch and he wrote: "I'm getting my ass handed to me and McGee thinks it's funny."

Dad wasn't laughing at Welch. But he was laughing at Syracuse head coach Paul Pasqualoni, who got so lathered up emotionally that he also got himself lathered up literally.

Dad

I said, "Paul, you have to calm down. There are TV cameras on us right now and you are slobbering all over yourself."

Some of the worst offenders weren't coaches at all. Ask any sideline official who worked a Miami Hurricanes game during the Jimmy Johnson era and they will tell you that the famously vocal head coach was never the foulest-mouthed man on The U sideline. It was the priest he always had there with him. The biggest mouth in the 1990 Orange Bowl wasn't that priest, but it was a Catholic. A Notre Dame reserve started stalking Dad along the sideline to shout his profanity-drenched complaints.

Sam

His white jersey was completely clean, just pristine. Clearly, he hadn't played, because we'd gotten to go down on the field the day before and realized it wasn't a field at all. It was dirt that was spray-painted green, so green paint got all over anyone who had been in the game. Hell, he might not have played all season.

Dad turned to him and said, "Son, do you really want to have to tell your grandchildren that you got thrown out of an Orange Bowl that you never even played in?"

But the headliners were and forever shall be the head coaches, especially the smart ones.

The 1986 regular season finale for Virginia Tech was a massive game for the Hokies, and for a couple of reasons. Bill Dooley was in his ninth and final season in Blacksburg, and a win against Vanderbilt at home would mean an invitation to the Peach Bowl in Atlanta on New Year's Eve. But Tech was struggling against the one-win Commodores. An early pass interference against Virginia Tech set Dooley off, immediately convinced that the SEC half of the split crew was out to screw over independent Virginia Tech. Then, when Dad and Booker didn't call a penalty against Vandy that Dooley believed they should have, he officially moved into meltdown status. The f-bombs were loud and frequent for a solid 10 minutes.

Booker and McGee, self-professed Bill Dooley admirers, finally agreed that enough was enough. Dad tossed his flag at Dooley's feet. Unsportsmanlike, 15 yards. Dooley froze and looked down at the flag. He couldn't believe it.

When Dad received his grades from the game, Bill Dooley had given him a 10 out of 10, but added on the comments line: "Jerry McGee cannot take constructive criticism."

Dad

I think back on those earliest conversations with Monte Kiffin at NC State. He was desperate to make it work, and came close to winning some big games. But he was fired not too long after that talk that we had in the locker room.

There is so much pressure on these coaches. Some guys thrive on that. But I think, even for them, it's hard for them to have any fun. Especially now versus back when I started.

In August 2016, I was in attendance for our annual summer preseason ESPN college football seminar. Every ESPN college football anchor, reporter, and analyst from TV, radio, the website, you name it, along with all of our producers, editors, and other bosses, we were all sitting in rows in one giant hotel ballroom. I found myself residing with the rules experts, a group of retired officials, as well as a couple of the conference and national coordinators, all there to answer any rules questions from the room. I sat next to Doug Rhoads, Dad's longtime crewmate. I had known him since I was a kid. He had just retired as the coordinator for the ACC and had joined ESPN to be an at-game rules analyst.

During the officials' panel Q&A session in front of the very large room, Rhoads suddenly found himself in a heated discussion with Al Groh, former longtime ACC coach (UNC, Wake Forest, Virginia, Georgia Tech) who had become an ESPN color analyst. Groh, apparently unhappy with the tone of the officiating panel, grabbed a hot microphone and started calling out the refs onstage, specifically addressing Rhoads. "You make these calls on the field, and there's no consequence for you! You get a call wrong in a big game, and it might cost me my job...DOUG!"

Rhoads, a former FBI agent and always the coolest guy in the room, smiled back at Groh and tried to defuse the situation. It worked, sort of. Groh left the room. When the session ended and Rhoads sat back down next to me, he leaned in and whispered, "You're probably the only guy in this room who knows this is about the 100th time Al and I have had a disagreement in front of a big crowd. That had nothing to do with today. I'm pretty sure he's still mad about a flag I had against him at Wake Forest in 1986." Then he winked. "It's pretty cool having a history like we do, isn't it? Not me and Al. Me and you."

You never know what exactly is going through a coach's mind or how long that thought (or grudge) might stick there, as they are constantly reshuffling their internal lists of that moment's priorities, while also constantly conjuring up new concerns, anything that might prevent them from winning that day's football game.

For example, take that 1990 Orange Bowl, the one that started with Lou Holtz's mystical all-knowing "where's the family sitting?" trick. The day before, there was a meeting held between representatives of Notre Dame; Colorado; NBC Sports, the producers of the halftime show; Orange Bowl executives; and the operators of the Orange Bowl Stadium, who gathered to discuss timing, spacing, ground rules, and any concerns about all of the above.

Sam

That field was terrible. It was like a painted fairway you'd find at a bad municipal golf course. This the biggest game of Dad's life. For the national championship. Our whole lives we'd wanted to see the Orange Bowl, with the Super Bowls and Miami Hurricanes games and all of those legendary games with Miami and Nebraska and Oklahoma we grew up watching.

We got to go into the stadium and walked around, taking pictures. We even got to see Notre Dame wrapping up their final practice.

But the place was a dump. It was cool. It was historic. But it was in bad shape. When we walked off the field, we had sand and green stuff all over our shoes. So, in my mind, when Dad comes out of this big logistics meeting that he has to attend, I'm thinking that the coaches of the two teams will have just raised hell about this terrible playing field. But that's not what they were worried about.

Dad

The meeting started to break up and Holtz kind of shouted to get everyone's attention. He says, "I have a question. How the heck does this work with the buffalo?" Everyone laughed and started leaving again. But he repeated himself. We all realized he was serious. He was talking about Ralphie, the Colorado Buffalo that they run down the sideline before every game. They had hauled his butt all the way from Boulder, so you knew they were going to run him. Holtz wanted to know exactly where and when that animal was going to be taking the field. He said, "What I don't need is for my All-American defensive star Chris Zorich to get run over before the game even starts!"

He had a great point. Now all of us who were going to be on the field were like, *This is a great question.* Now we wanted to know how this was going to work, too!

For Dad, the most notorious case of *pressurized coach plus dealing with problems no one knew about plus losing a game you shouldn't equals sideline explosion* took place on Halloween 1996. Boston College was visiting Pitt for a coveted Thursday night national showcase game on ESPN. The 4–4 Eagles were an 11-point favorite over the scuffling 2–6 Panthers. But BC never got into gear and lost an ugly contest 20–13.

In the middle of it all, Boston College head coach Dan Henning, a former NFL quarterback, two-time NFL head coach, and two-time Super Bowl–winner, totally and completely lost his mind.

Dad

Honestly, it escalated so quickly that it didn't seem real.

The back judge had a penalty against Boston College for 12 men on the field. We actually had some disagreement on that. I had counted, like I always did, and had 11, but the back judge was adamant and he was a good official, so the penalty stood. That triggered Henning, and as always, I was the guy who was right there next to him, so I was the one catching hell. At one point I even tried to explain, "Coach, if you'll notice, there's a flag on the field out there, but my flag is in my pocket." I was trying to let him know, stop screaming; certainly stop screaming at me.

For the next little while, he is following me up and down the sideline, just f-bomb after f-bomb, and finally he says, "My job is on the line, and you motherf--kers are out here half-assing the game..." and then he said something that ended up triggering me. "I don't know where the f--k they found you guys!"

Now I turned around and walked toward him. I said, "Well, I'll tell you where they found me! In a university president's office, where I work Monday to Friday. The question is where they found you. You're losing to Pittsburgh. On national television on Thursday night, with everyone in the country watching. If I was president at Boston College, you'd be looking for a job!"

I shouldn't have said that. And I wish that had been all that I said. I tried to walk away, but he followed me. He said something and when he walked away, I followed him. It was the only time I just lost the handle. But I was a university president now, and there was a lot of stress in my job, too. Football was supposed to be my stress release, but on a Thursday night, getting screamed at by this guy, who was supposedly known as a good guy, I just couldn't take it gracefully anymore.

Once it finally started to calm down, I looked over and I saw a kid holding a sideline microphone for ESPN. I said to him, "You didn't get all of that, did you?"

He didn't get all of it, but he absolutely got some of it. Most of the exchange had taken place during a TV timeout, so the nation didn't hear it. But I was two years into my entry-level career at ESPN, and at the Worldwide Leader in Sports we don't see commercial breaks during games on our air. The satellite feed that is beamed back to our offices is what we call the backhaul, a clean feed that includes everything at the stadium during those breaks when the viewing audience is watching ads or SportsCenter score updates. In the booth that night was play-by-play man Mike Patrick, a man with deep ACC roots, having called many of Dad's earliest TV games on Jefferson-Pilot back in the '80s. The sideline reporter was Dr. Jerry Punch, a coworker I knew very well.

This particular night I was in our ESPN Charlotte office. The only sound in the building was from BC at Pittsburgh, echoing throughout every room. But then, during this one commercial break, I heard a familiar sound that made me look up from my paperwork. Was that...Dad? And did he just drop an f-bomb?

I heard Doc Punch reporting to the production truck, not to be aired, but just in case it became a bigger problem once they returned from the commercials: "Guys, Coach Henning is really going at it with an official down here. That's the field judge. Dr. Jerry McGee. Ryan McGee's father."

In the closing moments of the game, Henning walked over to Dad. This time he didn't scream. "Jerry, if I offended you, I apologize."

"Me, too, coach. We both lost our cool, didn't we?"

Dad

That night neither one of us adhered to Mr. Neve's rule about watching what you said.

After the game, when cornered by a very nervous officiating coordinator, Dad refused to divulge the content of his conversation with Henning, saying only that they were having a disagreement over where to get the best steak in Pittsburgh after the game. In fact, he'd never fully explained what happened until now, not even to Sam or me.

Dad

I've never gotten into that much because I'm not proud of it. It was not my finest moment. Nor was it Dan Henning's finest moment. He didn't know the kind of stress I was under at my job. And, as we know now, that night we had no clue what a total and complete mess he was in the middle of at Boston College.

The following week, the entire nation knew. That's when Henning announced that he was suspending 13 Boston College football players for gambling. The game before Pitt, the Eagles had been crushed by Syracuse 45–17, and rumors were rampant in the Boston College locker room that some of the players on the team had placed bets on the game, against their own team. In the days leading up to the Pitt game, Henning held a team meeting to address those rumors and asked anyone who had bet on the Syracuse game to come forward. No one did. But as the night at Pitt turned ugly, so did Henning's mood. In the locker room after the loss, before leaving for the airport, he exploded on his team, promising that he would get the bottom of the gambling chatter. By the end of November, the county district attorney had become a regular in the BC football office, a campus gambling ring had indeed been exposed, eight Eagles were off the team permanently, and Henning would never coach college football again.

Dad

In the early 2000s, Dan Henning lived in Charlotte, not far from us. He was offensive coordinator of the Carolina Panthers. I used to wonder what would happen if we ran into each other at the grocery store. We never did.

Sam

I think, looking back, we understand why Dan Henning was in the frame of mind that he was that night at Pitt. But when he was calling the offense for the Panthers, if they had a bad day, I don't think any of us went out of our way to cut him much slack when it came to criticism.

By the way, there is no photograph of the Dan Henning versus Jerry McGee exchange on the Wall of Screaming. But there is videotape in the ESPN library. I know, I checked. Maybe I should have erased it.

TV Timeout
with Dr. Jerry Punch

"Hey Ryan, remember that deal between your dad and Dan Henning..."

It is October 11, 2014, a Saturday night, and I am talking to Dr. Jerry Punch at Charlotte Motor Speedway. The green flag for that night's NASCAR Sprint Cup Series race is still an hour away and we have taken up a position on pit road, where one of the race teams has set up a television to watch college football.

We are reminiscing about the mid-1990s, our earliest days working together, on a nightly ESPN2 auto racing show, *RPM 2Night*. I have always referred to him as "the other Dr. Jerry in my life," because I have worked with or alongside Punch for most of my adult life. He was always a hero of mine because he reported not only from college football sidelines, but also from the pits at NASCAR events and the Indianapolis 500. His was the dream job. He had been with ESPN since 1984, and I couldn't believe that I had been fortunate enough to work with him.

In 1996, we worked together nearly every Tuesday morning, shooting a recurring feature story that went behind the scenes at NASCAR race shops. We titled it Dr. Punch's House Calls. Cute, right? That gig included a shoot on the Tuesday morning following Dad's Thursday night throwdown with Dan Henning, an altercation I'd first gotten a heads-up on when Punch reported on it during a commercial break. He had also known Dad for a long time. So, the shock of seeing him completely lose his cool hadn't worn off. All these years later, I think it still hasn't. It certainly hadn't during this night in 2014.

"Ryan, I've been doing this for a while. I've seen some heated sideline arguments. I've seen some big arguments here at the racetrack between teams and officials. But I've never seen an argument go nuclear like that on both sides."

"Hey," Punch said, adding what he always has when we recall that night. "Do you remember what I asked you when I saw you that next week at our shoot?"

I remember. I will never forget it.

"I said, 'When we get done with this *House Calls* shoot today, let's pay your dad a house call at his office. I think we might need to check his blood pressure.'"

CHAPTER 7

GO (BIG) EAST,
YOUNG MAN

WHEN THE FINAL horn sounded on the 1990 Orange Bowl and the other New Year's Day games of 1990, it also signaled the end of the college football world as we knew it. The term "realignment" was being introduced into our collegiate sports lexicon.

During the December days leading into those games, the Big Ten offered a membership invitation to Penn State, the most successful independent college football program not named Notre Dame. It was Joe Paterno who had years earlier pitched the idea of his fellow eastern football independents joining forces with the membership of the Big East basketball conference. Now, with Penn State off the table and the Big Ten threatening to suck up all of the potential TV money from the region, the Big East moved quickly to do what JoePa had once dreamed of, expanding their league into the realm of football. Syracuse, Pitt, and Boston College were already solid football schools. When they went recruiting for football partners, they swung for the fences and stunned the sports world by landing Miami. The Canes were soon joined by fellow previously independent programs Virginia Tech, West Virginia, Temple, and Rutgers.

In 1991, the Big East would be playing football, and it needed football officials.

That job fell to Art Hyland, the Big East's legendary coordinator of basketball officials. He reached out to his member schools for recommendations, and Jerry McGee's name kept coming up, especially from Frank Beamer's staff at Virginia Tech. Same for Bill Booker. The best officials from the Northern independents were on board immediately. Talent from the South also signed on, especially when Hyland hired Dan Wooldridge to take over as Big East football officiating coordinator.

Wooldridge, a longtime basketball and football official with a career that included officiating the 1976 Olympics and being the first commissioner of the Old Dominion Athletic Conference, was an even-keeled Virginian, beloved throughout the sports officiating community. He quickly filled up the remaining slots on the roster Hyland had started.

There was a time when Dad could have never imagined leaving the ACC, but life was changing. I was out of the house, a student at the University of Tennessee, where I had landed a job working for the Volunteers football team on the film crew. Yes, I had figured out a way to get back into practices and press boxes. Sam would also be leaving for school soon.

Sam

Now my daughter is approaching the age when we need to start thinking about scheduling visits to college campuses, trying to determine where she might go to school, and Ryan is in the same boat. But the truth is that neither one of us really knows how to do that. When I started looking at colleges, I was looking at Virginia, North Carolina, Wake Forest, schools like that. Ryan was looking at places like Georgia, South Carolina, and Tennessee.

When it came time to visit schools, I think we both were like, "Hey, we've already been to all of these places, some of them a dozen times or more." Ryan probably would have never set foot on the campus in Knoxville if Dad hadn't had officiated the Duke-Tennessee game during Ryan's senior year of high school. I ended up at Wake Forest. By that time, I'd probably been to Wake at least seven or eight times for to watch Dad work football games. At least.

An emptying nest also meant that Mom could finally graduate from being our chauffeur, cook, schedule keeper, and nervous Saturday football TV viewing partner. She told me that she was very excited about the prospect of being free to hit the road with Dad more often, really for the first time. But she also admitted that she was a little worried that he might get his feelings hurt if she went with him on the game weekends, but chose to skip out on some of the actual games. It wasn't about football for her. It was about seeing different parts of the United States during the fall and experiencing that with Dad.

As for the football, Dad looked at the Big East schedule and ran it up against the ACC. It felt like a new day versus Groundhog Day.

Dad

At that time, the ACC schools were getting away from the big out-of-conference games. They'd started playing down. I was returning to a lot of games that I had already worked.

And there was an unwritten rule about postseason games that I thought was unfair. If you'd had two bowl games in a row, then you wouldn't get a third, no matter how high you'd graded out or how good of a season you'd had.

When I talked to the Big East, I asked them how they would determine bowl bids. They said the best at each position would go, period. Also, in addition to the eight Big East schools, their office would be assigning crews for Louisville, Army, Navy, and Notre Dame. With all of those schools, I was guaranteed a lot of games. And the chance to work Army-Navy? And guaranteed trips to Notre Dame?

I was never upset with the ACC. This was a chance to see new places and have new experiences, and at that stage of my life that was really the whole point of officiating for me, someone who loved college football.

So, I said yes.

The Big East experience wasn't a trip to another planet, but it was close. Out were the drives to Durham and Winston-Salem, replaced by Friday afternoon flights into Philly and Boston. The style of play was different, still very much tied to its old school granite-fisted Eastern football roots. There was a lot more artificial turf. The coaches and staffs were much more artistic in their use of curse words. And Dad's new crewmates, hailing largely from the northeastern corridor, certainly had a lot more vowels in their last names. During that first season I asked Mom about the Big East experience and she said, "It took me a couple of games to get used to all of the kisses to both my cheeks. I felt like I was in a *Godfather* movie."

It was a lot to process, but it was immediately fun. The only tension came from the blending of officials from so many different parts of the college football map. For the most part, everyone got along and enjoyed the cultural crash course. But there were those who definitely chose to draw a Mason-Dixon line between the North and the South.

Dad

I think that was inevitable. It was never widespread, but there was definitely some of that pretty early on. That first year of the Big East we had officials from 18 different states. Hell, we didn't know one another. Seven guys who came in from seven different cities on seven different airplanes, and now here we were on the field together to work Pitt at Ohio State or Michigan at Notre Dame or Rutgers at Texas.

We figured each other out pretty quickly, though. We had to. The good news was that Booker came with me. Bill had become my best friend in football, and we were going to get to experience this together.

They did so with smiles on their faces. Dad worked a whopping 13 games in 1991 and five on national television, a stunning number for the early 1990s, and that included the Army-Navy Game, held on the 50th anniversary of the bombing of Pearl Harbor. Over the course of the year he shared the field with nearly half of that year's New Year's Day bowl teams. During his seven years in the Big East, Dad averaged over a dozen games per season.

Sure, he had worked games with Penn State before, but those were on the road. Now he was walking onto the field in Happy Valley, with 96,672 fans chanting "We are!" He had been to Virginia Tech, but not this Virginia Tech of Beamer

Ball and half-smashed lunch pails. And yes, he had called games involving the Fighting Irish, but now he was actually in the House that Rockne Built.

Mom was in those places, too, and she was at the actual games most of the time. But where you could also find her was walking the New Jersey Boardwalk, having dinner atop Mt. Washington overlooking the Pittsburgh skyline, and riding the Maid of the Mist to the edge of Niagara Falls.

A few hours of being called a moron by a football coach and some fans? It felt like nothing more than a luxury tax.

Dad

What does the field judge do when it's time for the coin toss? You go get the captains. So, at Notre Dame I go to the locker room to get the captains, like I had done a hundred times. But then we started down the stairs, and I look up and there it is. The sign. "PLAY LIKE A CHAMPION TODAY."

To look up and see that…a little boy from Roberdell, North Carolina, doesn't think he's ever going to see that. And then you come out of the tunnel and take the players in their gold helmets to the 50-yard line, and standing across from you are the kids in their Michigan winged helmets. And then you see an older gentleman there for the game, and he looks familiar, and you realize, wait, that's Johnny Lujack. He won the Heisman when I was just a little guy. The first football I ever owned had his name on it. It got run over and flattened by a school bus. I cried until Daddy took me to the store to get a new football, and it had to be the Johnny Lujack model. And there he is, reaching out a hand to introduce himself.

Those first years in the Big East, it seemed like every weekend felt like that first trip to Clemson. Everything was new

and everything felt special. That's what I was hoping for when
I made that really difficult decision to leave the ACC.

The 1991 season was also the year that we McGees devised
a new way of consuming college football as a now-scattered
family. We did it over the telephone. I was chasing the Tennessee Volunteers, Sam was chasing the Wake Forest Demon
Deacons, and Mom was chasing Dad through the stadiums of
the northeastern corridor. That led to a never-ending series of
pre–cell phone era Saturday night and Sunday evening reports
on the three games we'd all attended over the weekend, or
breathless voice machine messages recorded as soon as we
returned home from those games.

That very year had started with perhaps the most memorable of those calls. I was at the Sugar Bowl in New Orleans,
a Tennessee student watching my team struggle with Virginia,
a team Dad had seen in person five times that season. Sam
had been with him for a couple of those games. On the Superdome jumbotron, they had just shown a highlight from the
Orange Bowl, a Notre Dame–Colorado rematch, again with
a potential national championship on the line. The crowd at
my game had been stunned into booing when we were told
that the thrilling 90-yard, final-minute, game-winning punt
return touchdown by Rocket Ismail had been called back for
a block in back. My college roommates immediately looked
at me and said, "Would Dr. McGee have called that?"

At the next timeout I rushed to a bank of payphones and
called home. With the cheering Sugar Bowl crowd booming
through the concrete concourse it was basically impossible
to hear anything on the other end. But once I could finally

make out Dad's voice yelling "NOPE!" I hung up and ran back to my seat.

I spent every autumn weekend following the Johnny Majors–led Volunteers around the SEC, the final couple of seasons as part of the team's film crew. In '91 alone I traveled to Cardinal Stadium in Louisville, Kentucky; Legion Field in Birmingham, Alabama; the Swamp in Gainesville, Florida; Commonwealth Stadium in Lexington, Kentucky; and also made my first trip to Notre Dame. I worked most of those games on the film crew, though several I attended by loading up my Pontiac Grand Am with roommates and buying a ticket off the street once we got there. Meanwhile, I spent every weekday afternoon at the practice field, so luckily assigned to be on the tower with Coach Majors, shooting videotape of practice while the legendary player and coach chatted me up about my schoolwork, told tales of his days as a near–Heisman Trophy winner, and opened every Monday practice by asking, "Where was your father officiating last weekend?"

At Wake Forest, Sam experienced one of the most magical seasons in the history of Demon Deacon football, coached by Bill Dooley, he of the "Jerry McGee cannot take constructive criticism" evaluation. The Deacs won eight games and the Poulan Weed Eater Independence Bowl over Oregon. On Halloween, Wake beat Clemson for the first time in 16 years. So, naturally, Sam and his friends tore down the goal posts.

Sam

We ripped off an upright and drove out of the parking with it sticking out the window of a Datsun. I bought a hacksaw and we set up shop in the middle of campus, sawing off pieces and selling them to classmates as they rolled the quad with toilet paper. Of course, as the proprietor of this enterprise, I saved the cap of the upright for myself. It's in my office.

The official start of college football season became the moment when Sam and I received the annual letter in our dorm room mailboxes containing the carefully handwritten composite "McGee Football Schedule" listing Tennessee; Wake Forest; Furman, Dad's new employer; NCAA Division II Wingate University; and, of course, "The Grey Ghost" himself. That jet-black head of hair from Dad's youth had long since given way to a head of silver that became his trademark.

Whenever we could figure out a way to be at the same game at the same time, we did, even if that meant doing a tiny bit of bending of the rules. When Dad got his '92 Big East schedule, it included Army at Wake Forest. Per the rules, Dad wasn't supposed to work a game of a school being attended by one of his children. But no one seemed to notice, so none of us pointed it out. It was an open date for Tennessee. So, there we were, me, Mom, and Sam, sitting in the stands and watching Dad together for the first time in in nearly two years.

Sam

Yeah, we kept that to ourselves. Other than bowl games, it was probably the only time we were able to watch a game together, three of us, like we had so many times before that. I think maybe I was worried that perhaps that chapter was over, that Ryan and I might move away after college, and who knew how often we'd be able to watch Dad's games together after that?

In the meantime, I used to love it when Dad couldn't work Wake Forest games, because I had a joke I would always pull. I would see who was working the game, and I always knew at least one or two guys on pretty much every crew. At least a couple of times it was Booker. So, I would leave my friends in the student section and go down the first row and call out to one of the officials during pregame. They would come over to the wall and we'd talk. Sometimes a couple of other guys on the crew would see us and they'd come over, too. Just catching up, small talk.

Well, my buddies in the student section, they would see this whole thing, me down there having a long talk with the officials. When I got back to the seats, I would say, real serious, "I talked to the refs. We're all set." If there was an early penalty against the other team, my friends would all look over at me and I'd just give them the thumbs up, like, "There you go. Our plan is coming together." Then I would give them the shush sign with my finger, like, "Y'all better not tell anyone what's happening here."

There was always concern in the backs of our minds that perhaps Sam was right. After school, once we'd both entered the real working world, would we also be finished birddogging Dad?

But we were all back together again sooner and much more often than we could have expected, though it didn't last long. Shortly after I graduated from Tennessee, I started at ESPN and moved to Bristol, Connecticut. One year later, Sam was admitted to Yale Law and moved down the road from me in New Haven. Both moves had impacts on our lives that we continue to benefit from to this day. But in the moment, all I could think was, *We're going to be able to go to some of Dad's games together!*

Sam

From our apartments in Connecticut, getting to Army or Boston College wasn't hard. Even if Dad wasn't working games there, we would have him ask the crew that was there to leave us tickets. Going to West Point in the middle of October, there's no place prettier than that. Or Boston College, for that matter. It was familiar, being there watching Dad, but the crowds were way different.

Ryan and I went to a West Virginia–Boston College game, and I don't think we considered ourselves to be naïve when it came to gambling, but that day we learned that we were. BC had trailed big the whole game. Toward the end they sent out the kicker, in, like, the last minute, and he kicked a meaningless field goal. Well, the crowd just went kind of crazy, booing and everything. We were like, "What the heck is going on with these people? So, you lost by 13 instead of 16, who cares?"

Then someone sitting by us explained that BC had just covered the spread. That wasn't something that would have gotten that kind of reaction at Georgia Tech–Duke.

What a time it was to be attending, let alone officiating, Big East football games. Curtis Martin was running the ball at Pittsburgh. Donovan McNabb was throwing it deep to Marvin Harrison at Syracuse. Jim Druckenmiller and Antonio Freeman were setting records at Virginia Tech. The coaches in the conference were West Virginia's Don Nehlen, Virginia Tech's Frank Beamer, Holtz at Notre Dame, and my coach, Johnny Majors, was back at Pitt after having been fired from Tennessee.

Then there was Miami. The 1991 national champs and '94 runners-up, coached by Dennis Erickson and then Butch

Davis, anchored by the likes of Heisman Trophy–winner Gino Torretta on offense, while Warren Sapp and then Ray Lewis powered the defense.

Dad

During all my years on the field, Ray Lewis was one of the players I interacted with most. Late in his final year at Miami, we had them up at Boston College. Ray didn't play much in that game. He was injured, and I think maybe he didn't play at all in the first three quarters. They were up by three and BC was driving late, trying to get into position to tie it up or maybe even win it. I look over my shoulder, and there's Ray, up off the bench and standing right behind me, watching the game.

I looked at him and said, "You gonna play?" He smiled back at me and said, "When it matters, I'll be out there." BC drove way down there and, sure enough, Ray ran past me with his helmet on. I think he made four straight tackles. Game over. See you later, boys, we're headed back to Miami.

There were absolutely those guys who, while the game was going on they were just a number on a jersey like everyone else, but when the game was over and you had a chance to sit down and really think about what you had just seen, and the players you had just watched, you knew who the special talents were. You looked at a guy like Ray Lewis and thought, he's not the biggest, strongest, or fastest guy out there, but he's clearly the best football player on the field. I'm not really an NFL guy. But there were absolutely guys who I watched as a fan after they went on to the NFL because of my experience with them in college. Ray Lewis was definitely one of those guys.

However, the most vicious hit that Dad saw in the Big East did not come from Ray Lewis. Actually, he didn't see it all. He felt it. The rest of us saw it. It was Pitt at Louisville, October 1, 1994.

These days, if you watch a University of Louisville game, you see a sparkling multimillion-dollar facility funded by Fortune 500 boosters and specifically built for big-time college football. In '94, the Cardinals were still trying to make it to that level, so they were still playing their games in a minor-league baseball stadium, with the rectangular football field crammed inside of the misshapen baseball diamond. The turf was terrible and the sideline was always very crowded, jammed with everyone from actual football personnel to photographers, university staff, and general hangers-on.

Dad

Billy West, the Pitt running back, had a huge season that year. Rushed for 1,300 yards. That day he broke a long run down the sideline, and I had it played perfectly. I was running backward, but I was in front of him, knowing he was going to go out of bounds at some point and I was going to have the spot marked as soon as that happened. That's always a tough place to be. You have to watch the players themselves, but you also have to be ready to spot where they go out of bounds, and when they are coming right at your feet like that, it happens all at once.

I think back on my career, almost all on the sideline, and how I wasn't hit all of the time is amazing. You develop a kind of automatic radar for trouble. I would go back and watch games on tape and there would be at least a couple of instances where I had danced around out of trouble, and I wouldn't even remember having done it.

But this time around, that's not what happened. The good news is that I got the call right. I got the play right. I got the spot right. Everything was right. The bad news is that with my eyes down, I never saw what was coming.

What was coming was West, a finely tuned teenage college athlete, weighing 205 pounds and covered in shoulder pads and a helmet, traveling at high speed. Sure enough, he had stepped on the line. Dad had his arms above his head giving a timeout signal while running in to make the spot. But a defender gave West a last-second shove while he was still on the move. The fifty-something university president, draped in nothing more than a polyester jersey, knickers, and a flimsy black ballcap, never stood a chance. Dad was hit so hard by West that his feet left the ground and he sailed several yards backward before landing on his right side and slamming down onto that over-worn artificial grass. This was old-school Astro-turf, maybe half an inch thick, tops, with a sheet of good old concrete beneath it. His unprotected shoulders hit first and then his head followed, snapping back and popping the back of his skull against that slab. Within a split second, he was surrounded by all of those people who had been crowding that sideline.

Dad

I'm pretty sure that more than a few of them thought I might be dead.

Jeff Triplette, the game's white hat who was about to leave college football for two decades as an NFL official, has since told me that he, too, believed that Dad would be leaving in an ambulance at best. The television audience certainly thought that. At the very least, they assumed that his back had been broken.

That audience included me and my brother.

Sam

I was in my senior year at Wake in my apartment with my roommates and we were doing what we did every Saturday. We were watching football, and specifically we were watching Dad's game. When that happened, my friends, who were not a quiet bunch, fell completely silent. It looked really bad.

I did not see the hit, but I did hear the reaction to it. I was barely two months into my first job at ESPN, production assistant, and my primary job those days was to watch games, log them, and then write and produce the highlights of those games for SportsCenter. You did that job in a room we called Screening, essentially an underground bunker. On a college football Saturday, it was an amazing room of noise and energy and excitement. There were literally dozens of games on TVs throughout this room with six just-out-of-college kids chattering and shouting and reacting to what was happening in those games.

My gig on this Saturday morning was not the Louisville game. I had been assigned another contest, sitting at a different screening station. When the hit happened, a huge groan went out from the corner of the room where Dad's game was being watched. Whatever, that happened all the time. But then the room fell silent. That never happened. Then someone from that corner said, very meekly, "Hey, McGee, you need to come over here. I think your dad just got his damn head knocked off."

Dad

Once the initial shock of the hit wore off, I was still laying there, kind of doing a checklist of my body. Nothing felt broken, but you can see on television that I immediately reached up and put my hands in my mouth.

When I saw that, on TV screen 900 miles away, I had the same thought as one of my coworkers, who said to me, "Oh damn, I don't think your dad knows where he is right now." But Dad still remembers all of it. He says he was fully aware of his surroundings, but when his head snapped back, his jaw had snapped shut with such force that he was convinced he had knocked out at least a few of his teeth. That's why he reached into his mouth.

Dad

Here's the most amazing part of the story. The first person to get down on the ground to see if I was okay was dressed in Louisville gear, and I assumed he was a team doctor or a member of the Cardinals athletic training staff. Turned out that he was a dentist. He just happened to be among that crowd on the sideline. Can you believe that? The one guy who could answer the one question that I had. *Were my teeth still there, and if they were, were they about to fall out?* He did a quick check, assured me that I was okay, and helped me to my feet.

Sam

He sat up and on TV you could clearly read his lips. He said, "Where's my hat?"

When he stood up and walked back onto the field, all my friends started cheering.

That's also what happened in Bristol, Connecticut. The most ironclad rule of being a member of the sports media has always been and will forever be that there is no cheering in the press box. But that day in ESPN screening, they were cheering Dr. Jerry McGee as he checked back into the game. One always-dramatic coworker compared it to Willis Reed, who returned to the court in Game 7 of the 1970 NBA Finals despite a torn thigh muscle to inspire the New York Knicks to victory over the Wilt Chamberlain and the Los Angeles Lakers.

Okay, it wasn't that. But it was still pretty badass.

I've been telling this story for 25 years to my friends and during speaking engagements. So, I've always believed that I knew the whole tale. But now, Dad has informed me that perhaps he wasn't as bulletproof as we'd always believed.

Dad

That night, instead of going to dinner with the crew, I decided to stay in my hotel room and order a pizza. I even talked the delivery guy into stopping somewhere on the way and buying some beer. This was several hours after the game. When the delivery guy arrived and I answered the door, he took one look at me and said, "Damn, man, are you the ref who got hit so hard in the game today?"

I told him, yeah, that was me, but I also asked him, how did he recognize me? No one ever recognized the officials out of uniform. He said, "But you're still in your uniform."

That's how out of it I was. I'd never changed. I had been sitting there all night on my hotel bed in my stripes and my knickers.

A couple of weeks later, Dad worked a game at Pitt, and as soon as he hit the field for pregame warmups Billy West threw his arms around the ref and apologized for almost committing an accidental murder. Pitt head coach Johnny Majors hugged Dad, too, and confessed that he had really been worried about him. Dad said thanks, but wondered why Majors' level of concern seemed so intense. Then the coach told Dad that throughout the remainder of the Louisville game, whenever they talked, Dad's answers never matched the questions Majors had asked him.

"Jerry, which of my players did you guys just call that holding penalty on?"

"Next week I'm working at Syracuse, Coach."

Once the applause and the pats on the back were through in the ESPN screening room, I suddenly realized that the game wasn't being carried on TV back home in North Carolina, so Mom likely had no idea what was happening. Right there at my screening station, I ignored my game to try and reach her before people started calling to tell her that her husband's neck

Young Sam McGee wore his dad's black referee hat 24/7, including on school picture day.

Growing up in Rockingham, North Carolina, Jerry McGee always had his Johnny Lujack football.

McGee family at 1990 Orange Bowl, No. 4 Notre Dame vs. No. 1 Colorado. (From left to right) Ryan, Jerry, Hannah, and Sam.

The good news? Thirteen-year-old Ryan captured Virginia's Barry Word scoring the game winner. The bad news? Ryan was run over one second later.

Part of every official's pregame checklist—locating the family in the grandstands. Jerry has just spotted the McGees at the 1990 Orange Bowl.

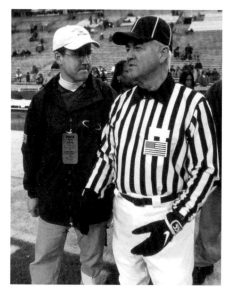

Ryan and Jerry together on that same Virginia sideline 19 years later. (Les Stone)

Dad has hit a career milestone, celebrating with Sam, Ryan, and Hannah. The office had a referee-themed cake made for the occasion.

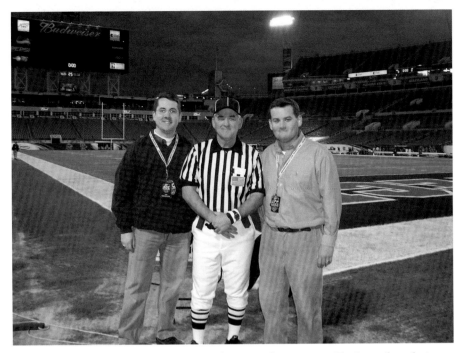

Ryan, Jerry, and Sam at inaugural ACC Championship in 2005. The boys thought it was Dad's last game. It was not.

Ryan doing his best to embarrass mother, Hannah, at 1996 Holiday Bowl—and doing a fine job of it.

Jerry McGee's officiating photos on display in his Charlotte, North Carolina, home, also known as The Wall of Screaming.

The Wall of Screaming features, among other shots, South Carolina's Joe Morrison expressing some displeasure during the '84 Clemson game...

...Mike Shula with a question about a call during Duke vs. Alabama in 2006...

...and this isn't merely a photo of Jerry McGee and Lou Holtz, ref and coach. It's a pair of emotionally struggling husbands.

October 1, 1994, McGee's Willis Reed moment, blasted through the air at Louisville, but reentering the game. "Where's my hat?" (WDRB-TV)

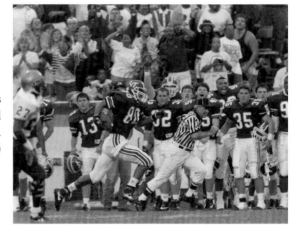

McGee racing Virginia Tech's Antonio Freeman to the goal line in 1992. (Virginia Tech Athletics)

Chasing USC's Dwayne Jarrett on a 62-yard touchdown catch and about to flag the Michigan defender for a personal foul in the 2007 Rose Bowl. (USC Athletics)

The best part of the gig is the friends made along the way. The inseparable duo of Bill Booker and Jerry McGee.

McGee and longtime ACC colleague Doug Rhoads at Duke in 1984, during the ACC officials' (thankfully) brief shorts experiment.

The "Virginia Crew" of 1998, McGee's favorite season on the field. The men who also helped him get through the grief of '99.

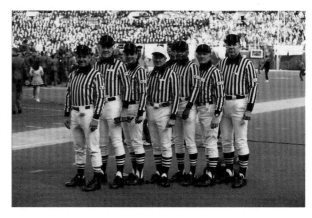

There was no greater honor in McGee's career than working the 1991 Army-Navy Game, held on the 50th anniversary of Pearl Harbor.

The 2007 Rose Bowl crew meeting grand marshal George Lucas. The Star Wars–obsessed McGee sons are still jealous of this.

Pregame laughs with line judge Rick Page, referee Jack Childress, McGee, and umpire Clark Gaston. Nearly a century of combined college officiating experience in this photo. (Les Stone)

Jerry McGee in the final minutes of the 2009 BCS Championship, conversing with Ryan on the sideline as the career ticks down.

From his first big-time conference game to the antics of Danny Ford to the Bowden Bowl, Clemson's Death Valley is home to many of Jerry McGee's fondest memories.

Forever the Field Judge.

was broken or that he no longer had any teeth. She was audibly relieved when I said that he was okay. But she was audibly conflicted when I told her that he was back in the game.

"But Mom," I said, "the man who was already my hero has just now done the impossible. He made a room full of hardened sports fanatics actually cheer for the guy they grew up hating. A damned referee."

Sam

I have always taken a lot of pride in that, making people whose first instinct is to always run officials down, making them start to double-clutch on that little bit. I'm not an idiot, so I know how people are generally always going to feel about officials. Most people don't care for them by nature. But if I can make them start watching that third team on the field, even just a little, and understand that those guys are out there getting booed and hit and called all sort of names, but still work as hard as they can to protect the integrity of the rules, only because they love the game so much...if I can make someone understand that even just a tiny little bit, then that's a win.

That mission means forcing education on rooms full of football watchers, whether they want that lesson or not. And yes, that strategy applied to my time in ESPN Screening, just as it applies to my time in the press box now as a sportswriter. You know the one guy in the room who says the one thing that causes everyone else to scream in unison, "Okay, we got it! Now shut up!"? Yeah, that's totally me.

Back in those early days at ESPN, when a big play in a big game would dominate the entire campus, I would always make sure everyone knew it if there had actually been two big plays. Let's say Randy Moss would break off a 75-yard touchdown reception for the Minnesota Vikings. Just as the volume of the reaction in Screening was dying down, I would shout "He beat everyone to the goal line, but not the back judge," often to a wadded-up piece of paper being winged off my head. During the most recent College Football Playoff National Championship in New Orleans, I excitedly spent an entire TV timeout pointing to the Pac-12 officiating crew as they huddled, explaining to my ESPN.com coworkers that the white hat was having to also referee an argument among his crewmates, the officials from one side of the field clearly irritated that a personal foul had been flagged on their sideline from an official who was all the way on the other side of the Superdome floor.

As always, my press box colleagues indulged me. But I totally saw their side-eyes.

Sam

To me, if you're going to be one of those people who just rips officials all the time, wouldn't you want to be educated on what they really do and how they do it? If people got tired of me talking about Dad and where he was officiating that weekend, then okay. But none of my close friends did. They enjoyed the college football more because of it. I know they watched games that they wouldn't have otherwise because of it.

Say, the 1993 Peach Bowl in Atlanta. If Dad's recovery from his concussion at Louisville was his Willis Reed NBA Finals moment, then this night was his version of Michael Jordan's "Flu Game," officiating a boxing match of a football game while also running a fever. Clemson escaped with a win over Kentucky, via a fumbled red zone interception that still haunts Wildcats fans to this day. But what we remember most about that night was the fact that it was one of the first major sporting events in the year-old Georgia Dome, and that referee Al Hynes damn near shattered the fiberglass roof of the building when he forgot to turn off his microphone after announcing a penalty, blowing his whistle into that microphone, over the dozens of massive public address speakers and directly into the eardrums of the 63,416 people in attendance.

Or, the 1995 Plymouth Holiday Bowl between Colorado State and Kansas State, a Rocky Mountain team that was always pretty okay against a midwestern squad that had always been pretty awful. What we know now is that K-State was in the early stages of an incredible era of success under Bill Snyder, and that two young assistants in the game, Snyder's defensive coordinator Bob Stoops and Rams wide receivers coach Urban Meyer, would one day become Hall of Fame head coaches. But that night, all the McGee family knew was that the San Diego Zoo was awesome and so was Holiday Bowl grand marshal and original Mercury 7 astronaut Wally Schirra. I know this because I basically ran out into traffic during the Holiday Bowl parade to shake his hand. I also thought it was awesome to pose with my mother for photos as I wore a green and yellow Colorado State pom-pom on my head like a wig. I don't think she thought it was as awesome as I did.

But it didn't take any encouragement from any McGees to convince our friends and family to watch Dad's next postseason game, the 83rd edition of the Rose Bowl Game, played on

January 1, 1997, between the No. 4 Ohio State Buckeyes and the No. 2 Arizona State Sun Devils. If ASU and its showman quarterback Jake "the Snake" Plummer won the game, they would also win at least a share of the national title, their first in 100 seasons of trying.

Sam

This was Dad's 10th bowl game. We count Army-Navy as a bowl game. The Big East assigned it like it was, and he'd had it twice. He had also worked two Gator Bowls; the Peach, Citrus, and Holiday Bowls; an Orange Bowl that had determined a national championship; and the year before this one, he'd worked Notre Dame and Colorado again in the Fiesta Bowl.

Those are great games. But they aren't the Rose Bowl.

I'm not sure we ever saw my mother so excited. From the time we landed at Burbank's Bob Hope Airport, deplaning via open air steps with a backdrop of the Hollywood Hills, she started smiling and never stopped. We went to Disneyland with Mom's niece and my cousin (she made Dad stay back at the hotel because he was in "bowl game mode"). We strolled the streets of Pasadena. We attended the pre–Rose Bowl luncheon with the teams, marching bands, and grand marshals Carl Lewis and Shannon Miller. And, most importantly, we went to the Rose Bowl Stadium the evening before the game. We were allowed to step inside the empty bowl, and this time there was no Orange Bowl-ish disappointment. The place was a living postcard. But Mom rushed us through it. She wasn't there to gawk at the playing field or even the thousands of Arizona State fans, camped out NASCAR infield–style in the lot surrounding the stadium.

Nope, she was headed straight for the floats. Hundreds of people were frantically gluing rose petals to the giant mobile parade floats, sculpted into the shapes of birds, landscapes, and even sci-fi characters. Never one to take a lot of pictures, Mom snapped away. At one point, she looked at me and said, "If I crawl up into one of these floats, you think they would let me spend the night here watching them finish these for tomorrow morning?" The next morning, we were sitting on that parade route. While the tickets allotted to the families of officials for games were never great, these seats were incredible. We could hear Bob Eubanks talking from his TV broadcast perch right behind us.

"How many times in my life have I watched this on TV, and here it is," Mom said at one point, not caring a bit that it was overcast and drizzly. "It doesn't seem real, does it?" She sounded exactly like Dad when he talked about taking the field at places like the Orange Bowl, Georgia, Notre Dame, and, just a few hours later, the Rose Bowl.

If you will recall, we mentioned earlier in this book that Dad had three plays he's never been able to shake. You already know about the onside kick at UNC-Maryland '83, the call people still bring up all the time. You've also learned of the BYU touchdown in the '85 Citrus Bowl, the one he still thinks he got wrong, but we still think he got it right.

Now you will learn about that third play, the one that lives somewhere in between those first two. Some people still bring it up. Some people still think he got it wrong. But we still think he got it right.

Because Sam and I are mean, we recently invited Dad into my basement, fired up YouTube, cued up the play, and watched it with him, revisiting the '97 Rose Bowl with a little over 10:00 remaining in the second quarter. Arizona State, trailing

7–0, had the ball at Ohio State's 25-yard line. After the snap, Plummer pulled off a beautiful pump fake and then went deep, toward the left front corner of the end zone. His target was wide receiver Ricky Boyer, who was covered tightly by Buckeyes cornerback Antoine Winfield.

Boyer left his feet at nearly the 5-yard line, flying through the air behind Winfield, over the pylon, and right past Dad, casually walking by the 1-yard line because his mechanics had him in the right position as the play came toward him.

Suddenly, a whole lot happened at once. Boyer, his arms completely outstretched, grabbed the ball with his fingertips, and he and a flailing Winfield hit the grey-painted grass with a thud, both rolling and popping up as Dad stepped into the end zone behind them and signaled touchdown.

Dad

Now...freeze it [the video is at the very moment Boyer's fingertips are touching the football]. Today, this is an easy call. It's incomplete. In the middle of all this debate over what is or isn't a catch, you have to hold the ball a lot longer now than you used to. But back then, if you had possession of the ball even for a brief time, you had possession of it, especially when you are down there at the goal line.

On our TV, Boyer is frozen over that goal line.

Dad

The call, when I made it, wasn't that hard to me, because if I stick that ball over the goal line, that's a touchdown. You can even slap it out of my hand now and it doesn't matter. In the end zone, if you have possession and your foot hits the ground, it's a touchdown.

Dad walks to the TV and points to Boyer's left foot. His right leg has been crashed into by Winfield and is back in the air, but his left toe is on the turf.

Dad

Again, today this is a different call. But on this day, all that had to happen was that he had possession of the ball and his foot touches the ground, no matter how much a split-second it is for. Now, hit play…

It indeed does all take place in a split-second. The touch of the ball, the toe touching the ground, and the hand with the football crashing into the ground right behind it. On the two replays that follow, color commentator Dick Vermeil points to the hands hitting the turf, saying that Boyer had trapped the ball against the ground and so he believed it wasn't a catch.

That's what the audience at home heard. It's also what the folks in the press box heard, including Big East officiating coordinator Dan Wooldridge. The Ohio State–slanted crowd in the bowl itself also didn't like what it had seen on the replays featured on the end zone big screen.

Dad

I was never worried about it. My only thought when I determined that he had caught the ball was, what hit the ground first? His foot or his hands? I knew his foot had hit first.

It's fascinating to think about the college football world as it was on January 1, 1997, versus what it is today. When Dad made that call, there was no replay booth or conference replay command center. Instant replay of any kind wouldn't debut in the college game for another seven years. The 2020 Rose Bowl telecast on ESPN utilized nearly 50 cameras, all set to the newest level of high definition and including cameras mounted in goal line–pylons. In 1997, ABC Sports used less than a quarter of that camera count and the idea of a Pylon Cam would have sounded like something taken from the Jetsons.

In other words, the officials back then were operating without a safety net. When Dad tells today's up-and-comers about those times and those games—like this, a touchdown in arguably the biggest game he'd ever worked—those youngsters get the shakes just thinking about it.

Dad

At halftime of the game, Dan says to me, "I don't know, I think we might have missed that catch on the touchdown." It was the first time I even thought of worrying about that. It wasn't on my mind in the second half of the game; there was too much to do to worry about something that had already happened. But as soon as it was over, I was like, dammit, do I need to be worried about this?

Arizona State did not win the Rose Bowl or a national title, though it seemed like they were going to both. Plummer scored on a snake of a play to make the score 17–13 with only 1:40 remaining in the game. But ASU inexplicably came back with a short kickoff, setting up a 65-yard game-winning touchdown drive for Ohio State. During that drive, Arizona State was flagged for pass interference twice, including one call from Dad. There was nothing controversial about those muggings. His only criticism of the crew watching that final drive in my basement?

> **Dad**
>
> I believe we could have called a third one.

The flight back to North Carolina wasn't unlike the '85 drive back from the Citrus Bowl. Dad needed to get home to see the videotape.

> **Sam**
>
> Again, we thought it was the right call, but Dad was not convinced. The exchange with Dan certainly hadn't helped. But we also reminded him that no one else on the crew had disputed it. He still wasn't happy about it. The video of the play, we watched it so many times, and it was close.

Thank goodness for *Sports Illustrated*.

Later that year, long after the Rose Bowl game, *Sports Illustrated* published a "Best Photos of the Year" type of spread. In it was a two-page photo sequence of Arizona State's Ricky Boyer, body outstretched, with his fingers spread out over the back of the football and his left toe stuffed into the end zone turf. The image was captured in literal space of an eyeblink. But oh, what an image it is.

It has hung on Dad's wall ever since, but not on the Wall of Screaming. It occupies its own special place, as it should. Particularly if any complaining Ohio State fans come around.

A decade after that, I was working at NASCAR Productions (think NFL Films, but with racecars). A coworker across the hallway was a former Arizona State athletics employee and always said he was pals with Plummer, who by then was the starting quarterback of the Denver Broncos. One day I walked into his office and, lo and behold, he had the Snake on speakerphone.

"Jake!" my coworker shouted into the phone. "The guy from the office next to me just walked in. His dad was one of the referees in the Rose Bowl!"

"That's cool. Did he make any big calls in that game?" Plummer asked through the speaker.

"Yeah," I replied. "He had that crazy touchdown catch in the front corner of the end zone in the first half."

"Good call," Plummer said.

"But he also had one of the pass interference penalties against you guys on that final drive."

"Oh. Well, screw this."

The line clicked. The Snake was gone.

Dad

When I wear my bowl rings or a bowl watch on a trip or somewhere, and it happens to catch someone's eye, they will ask what it is and where it's from. As soon you mention the game, some people's eyes will light up. It makes you think, for a split-second, oh man, if this guy is a real Colorado fan or an Arizona State fan, or whomever, they might try to push me out of this plane!

Dad's last bowl watch earned during his Big East days came from the 1998 Florida Citrus Bowl, when Steve Spurrier's Florida Gators defeated Paterno and Penn State 21–6. In seven seasons he had worked seven postseason games, two Kickoff Classics, and been everywhere from Austin to Columbus to Tulane. But at season's end, Dan Woolridge retired as the Big East coordinator. He had managed to keep the simmering Mason-Dixon Line tension from becoming a real issue. But then Dad was tipped off by one of his dearest friends among the Northerners that one of the guys who had always seemed bitter about North vs. South was going to marginalize anyone with a Southern accent as soon as he was put in charge.

Dad

No matter what you do for a living, there will always be people who have decided that if you got an opportunity they didn't, well, it couldn't possibly be because they hadn't earned it, right? It had to be politics. In this case, the Southern guys taking care of the Southern guys. That was never the case. Anyone who thought that Dan was cutting me slack because I was from the South certainly didn't see our discussions that night at the Rose Bowl. The highest-rated guys went to the bowl games, just like Dan had promised. I officiated football because of my love for the game, and I certainly didn't need any extra drama in my life.

I had worked with some great officials in the Big East, and many have remained treasured friends. But it was pretty obvious where this was going. So, with that writing on the wall, I started looking for a new conference. Gerry Austin was now the coordinator of Conference-USA, so I was talking to him. I had discussions with several conferences.

But before I committed, I called Bradley Faircloth at the ACC. Ernie Cage, one of the most beloved downfield officials in the history of the conference, had just passed away after a heroic battle with cancer. So, Bradley needed an experienced guy. He suggested we spend the weekend thinking about it. The next week he called and invited me back, but he promised nothing. I said yes.

Then I had to go home and tell Hannah.

Mom was pissed. Like, Dan Henning–level angry. When Dad and Booker moved to the Big East in '91, it had stung a lot of their ACC colleagues. But Booker, citing the rigors of Big East travel, had returned the ACC after only one year. He had long ago mended his fences, but there was still anger at Dad for leaving the club.

As a family, the last time we had seen Bradley Faircloth was just a couple years earlier, at the beach. He had coincidentally rented a house next door, and when Dad walked over to say hello, Faircloth had stared at him, ignored him, and driven away.

Mom had never forgotten that. She said, "How can you go back and work for him?!"

Dad

It was a fair question. But I had missed my friends in the ACC. I wanted to hang out with those guys again.

We had no idea how badly Dad was going to need them.

Players' Timeout
with Ray Lewis

"Your dad is the Doc I used to talk to on the field?!"

It is winter time in Bristol, Connecticut, the dark, snow-buried days that always close out one year and start the next. I am in the SportsCenter newsroom, the always-bustling nerve center of the ESPN campus, where college bowl games are on countless TVs around the room. I am discussing one of those games with Ray Lewis, who is in town as an NFL analyst. His Miami Hurricanes have just lost, and he isn't happy about it. We talk about The U, past versus present. That leads to talking about his time at The U. And that leads, naturally, to talking about Dad sharing the field with Lewis during his college playing days.

When someone does remember Dad, it's typically a coach or a staff member, the people he worked alongside for years. Players aren't around very long. I suppose all officials look pretty much the same to most people, but especially teenagers who are a little busy during game days.

But when I recall the "You gonna play?" story from Boston College, perhaps the most intimidating eyes in football history light up. Lewis tells me about the first time they met, when the Miami coaches invited a group of Big East officials to fly in for a Saturday scrimmage and also hold a rules session to answer any questions the Hurricanes players might have ahead of the 1995 season. When the officials were introduced, their day jobs were also announced. "Dr. Jerry McGee, field judge, he's the president at Wingate University in North Carolina."

Lewis saddled up to Dad and said, "Man, you ain't no college president out here refereeing football!'"

Dad responded, "Then you ain't no linebacker."

Lewis laughed. "Oh, I am *definitely* a linebacker!"

"The next day at practice we talked some more," Lewis remembers. "Some of it was smack. But most of it was real football questions. What's he looking for on penalties? What's my best argument going to be with a referee if I really think I am being wronged? From then on, we had a running conversation for like two years. I knew he wasn't going to give me anything just because I thought we were boys, just like he knew I wasn't going to not play as hard as I could just because we had had a conversation about what I maybe could or couldn't get away with. It was like a teacher. They are going to help you do your best, but they are still going to grade you the same as everybody else."

Ray Lewis tells me it always made him smile when he saw Dad was on the field for a Miami game. I tell him Dad always felt the same way.

"By the way, that day at Boston College, when he asked me if I was going to play, you know what I said. 'Oh, I am *definitely* going to play!' And I did, didn't I?"

CHAPTER 8

LOVE THE GOOD DAYS,
OWN THE BAD ONES

W HEN DAD RETURNED to the ACC in 1998, his schedule wasn't the best he'd ever worked, but it was also far
from bad. The conference had five teams ranked the AP Top 25
during the season and Dad's crew saw all five of them at least
once. The top team was Florida State, led by Peter Warrick and
Chris Weinke and on its way to the inaugural BCS Championship Game.

Dad had indeed received the cold shoulder from more
than a few of his ACC colleagues at the summer rules clinic.
When it was time for a veterans-only meeting, he was asked
to leave the room with the other rookies. He also knew that as
a de facto rookie he wouldn't be receiving a bowl assignment
at season's end. But despite all of that, he still remembers '98
as the most fun he ever had in college football.

Dad

They called us the "Virginia Crew" because five of the seven
of us lived there. They were all old-school ACC guys, and none

of them were mad at me about the Big East thing. I was back with Booker again. Tom Lock, Doug Rhoads, and Bud Elliott, too. So, two guys who were on my very first ACC crew in 1983 and my best friend. Robin Wood was the referee, a UVA Law grad who'd been in the ACC since 1975. Watts Key was the side judge, and I think he was in his 10th year in the league.

Key was lovingly known by many in the ACC as "Snake Bite." One year, when he was studying his rulebook on his back deck, he stepped into his backyard to quiet his overexcited dog. The dog was worked up over a snake, a fact Key didn't realize until after the copperhead had already struck the side judge in the foot. Rhoads once told me the story and said that Key's foot "swelled up like a damn watermelon." He didn't miss the football season, but the injury did excuse him from the summer clinic and the universally dreaded timed one-mile run. "I think some of the guys thought it was all just a scheme to get out of the mile run," Rhoads explained, laughing. "So, from then on he was 'Snake Bite.'"

Sam

The Big East was great, but it had taken some time for us to learn the new names and who was a good guy and who was not, all of that. When Dad went back to the ACC, we instantly knew everyone again. We knew their backstories. It was like we had never lost touch, because while Dad was gone, we were still watching plenty of ACC football and every bowl game, and there were all of the old ACC guys.

When Dad got back with those guys, it was like getting back together with your old college friends. The real friends, where no matter how long you were gone, you just picked back up right where you left off.

Dad

It wasn't just those guys, either. I was going back to Clemson and North Carolina and Maryland, all of the places where I worked so many games before. The coaches and the players were different at most of them, but the chain crews were the same. The security guys. The trainers who were taping my ankle. They were all still there.

As were the comedy stylings of Booker and McGee.

Somewhere on the road, the crew decided to have their pregame meeting at the hotel, in Dad and Booker's room. Before the others arrived, Booker made one of the beds, but only one. During the meeting, their crewmates kept looking over at the two beds, one that had obviously been slept in and the other looking like it hadn't been touched.

Dad

Finally, someone spoke up and said, "Did you guys sleep in the same damn bed last night?" I said, "Hell guys, we always sleep in the same bed. I get cold."

All of the worry that Hannah and I had about what might happen if I came back to the ACC, it disappeared fast. It was like that day at Wake Forest in 1983, when she talked about the smile I had on my face, being with my friends, and how much she loved that.

But she never forgave Bradley Faircloth.

It was a year of transition for the entire family. In May, Sam married Marci Timm, a college athlete who grew up in Florida Gators country and graduated high school with Miami Hurricanes legend Warren Sapp. I committed the ultimate college football sin and got married on an autumn Saturday, November 21. My bride was Erica Allen, who'd grown up in Knoxville, attending games at Neyland Stadium and whose mother had gone to Georgia games as a teenager, traveling up from Savannah with Uga the Bulldog mascot riding in her lap. The weekend after our wedding, Dad and the Virginia Crew worked a classic edition of their state's biggest rivalry, a top 20 Commonwealth Cup showdown won by Virginia over Virginia Tech 36–32.

Without a bowl game to work, Dad accepted an invitation to officiate in an NCAA Division II All-Star event, the January 9, 1999 Snow Bowl, played in Fargo. The attraction was to have Dad, president of a Division II university, come give a speech and officiate the game. Doug Rhoads once said to me, "How bad was that hit at Louisville, really? Because he had to have suffered some sort of brain damage to voluntarily fly into North Dakota in January."

Dad

I have never laughed as much as I did during the 1998 football season. Never. We officiated the heck out of every game and we loved being together.

Unfortunately, the laughter stopped on February 28, 1999. Mom and Dad were on a much-needed sabbatical in the Caribbean when Mom woke up in the middle of the night complaining of a headache. In no time at all, she was gone, having suffered a fatal brain aneurism.

She was only 54.

Dad

Hannah McGee went to the Gator Bowl, two Citrus Bowls, the Orange Bowl, and the Rose Bowl. She went to Virginia, Ohio State, Notre Dame, Clemson, all of the Tobacco Road schools. She saw some of the biggest games in college football history.

I think about how I would make sure I knew where the tickets were and then make sure I spotted her from the field and stopped to wave at her. Usually, the boys were sitting right there with her, from the time they were these little guys all the way up until they were married young men.

What an image.

There is a beautiful line that Bruce Springsteen has used when describing the death of his longtime saxophonist and on-stage wingman, Clarence Clemons. When asked what life would be like not having the Big Man around, The Boss said that was like being asked what life would be like without the rain.

When Mom passed away, it was the opposite of that. It started raining the morning of her funeral and I swear it didn't stop for six months, an emotional downpour so thick that it choked us all. It was dark. It took away our ability to see anything around us. It created perpetual disorientation. When that is what your world has suddenly become, drenched in grief, you find yourself desperately squinting and reaching into that darkness, hoping for any tiny speck of light, hope, something to grab ahold of. Something to tell you that it is okay to finally take one step forward.

As autumn '99 drew closer, it was football that appeared as that light for the McGee family.

The summer rules clinic had always meant a time of fellowship. Now it meant badly needed hugs, handshakes, and company. The arrival of Dad's game assignments had always meant so much to our entire family, the list of what games and where they would be played and how long before we finally got to go. Now the delivery of the schedule meant target dates, something to look forward to. Actually, 12 somethings to look forward to.

Sam

Football was always the escape, but before 1999 it had been an escape from work. Now it was an escape from everything. You hear athletes talk about stepping between the white lines and nothing else matters, only that game and that moment, right there.

Dad needed to get back in between those lines.

The season started with the No. 1 team in the nation, Florida State, starting a season that would see them run wire-to-wire, all the way to a national title. From Tallahassee and Chapel Hill to Morgantown and Clemson, the coaches and support staffers with whom Dad had reconnected upon his return to the ACC the year before were now all waiting in impromptu sideline receiving lines, eager to offer up their support. And he needed all of them.

When it got to be too much, the Virginia Crew would run interference, trying to let Dad enjoy his fall Saturdays instead of being saddened by them. Booker was essentially his body-guard, deflecting well-intended mourners when he needed to and keeping Dad laughing whenever possible. When we all made the trip to the 1990 Orange Bowl, Booker's father had just passed away a few days before. I had no idea. And why was that? Because Dad made it his mission to protect his friend and ensure that the game was the great experience it was supposed to be. Now, nearly a decade later, Booker was returning that favor.

At season's end, Booker wasn't selected for an on-field position in a postseason bowl game, but when Dad earned a trip to the Liberty Bowl, Booker accepted a job as the alternate official for that game, just so that he could travel to Memphis and keep an eye on Dad.

Sam

My wife and I made the trip to that Liberty Bowl. Booker was always the one who was going to instigate a good time, but on this trip, he was especially dangerous, because unless something went very wrong, he wasn't going to be officiating in the game, and because he was working so hard to cheer Dad up.

At the hotel, there were two hospitality rooms set up. At bowl games there was usually one set up for the officials and there was at this game, but it was pretty bad. It was just a room with some chairs in it. But the hospitality room next door was completely stocked with liquor. Booker walked in there and looked at the bar, looked to see if anyone was around, and said, "Man, this is nice in here, isn't it, Sam? Help me carry it into our room."

The game was played on New Year's Eve. It was a weird matchup, and Southern Miss beat Colorado State. But that night it was New Year's Eve and it was Y2K. People thought all the computers were going to shut down and all hell was going to break loose. Dad and my wife, Marci, were both really sick. I'm not sure how Dad even worked the game. But there was no way I wasn't going to see Beale Street the night that the world was going to end. I dragged them down there and I met this crazy guy in a purple zoot suit and we went dancing down Beale Street screaming "Happy New Year!" and stuff about Y2K. Marci and Dad just sat there and waited on me, patiently.

It was a release. It was a great time, and that year hadn't had many.

By the way, I am happy to report that the next day, the world had not ended.

Dad

And I am happy to report that 1999 was finally over.

"Ryan, you've never seen anything like that season," Doug Rhoads once told me, recalling the way that the college football community had embraced Dad, hoping to help him. Rhoads had endured a similar experience years earlier, when his son, Randy, was killed in an accident during his college spring break. I had befriended Randy on ACC sidelines in the 1980s. I even snapped a photo of him during a Maryland-Duke game in '86, crouched along the sideline at Wallace Wade Stadium, intensely watching his dad.

Rhoads said of Randy and Mom, "If you can live through losing a son, or a wife, then being called an idiot by a football coach because you might have missed a pass interference call? That's a damn cakewalk, man. But after those tragic losses, you know who were among the first people to keep checking on me, or who kept checking on your father? Those same guys who called you an idiot."

Dad

For 30-plus years, when I officiated football, deep down I really thought that football needed me.

In 1999, I realized how wrong I had been. I realized that I needed football.

Coach's Timeout
with Lou Holtz

"You know, I like to joke about that photo, but the reality is that this image tells a much different story than anyone outside of a very few of us were aware of."

It is summer 2013 and I am showing Lou Holtz a photograph on my phone. The College Football Hall of Famer has been retired from coaching for nine years. We are at ESPN's annual preseason college football seminar, sitting together during a lunch break, the TV analyst and the sportswriter.

It's the photo from Dad's Wall of Screaming, the one from the 1999 Clemson–South Carolina game, when Dad is on his way to deliver bad news to Holtz, his head buried in his hand. This is the picture that Holtz had kidded about, saying that in the final game of a winless year he was thinking, "Now, where exactly am I going to take my wife, Beth, on vacation once this season is finally over?"

"But look at us both," Holtz is saying now. "These are two men who are just trying to make it to tomorrow."

From a purely football standpoint, 1999 is the year that Lou Holtz returned to coaching and endured an 0–11 year. But in addition to rebuilding the Gamecocks program, he had also been taking care of his wife. That season, Beth Holtz was in the middle of a years-long bout with throat cancer that pushed her through a ringer of more than 80 chemotherapy treatments and multiple surgeries.

So, the two men in that photograph aren't just a football coach and a football official. There are a widower and a husband of a cancer fighter. Before that game they had talked. Holtz said he was so sorry about Mom, the woman whose name he had so impressively recited from memory on the Orange Bowl sideline a decade earlier. Dad told Holtz how amazed he was at the strength of their family, including assistant coach Skip Holtz, in the face of their wife and mother's cancer battle.

"That whole year people asked me how in the world and why in the world would I keep coaching while Beth was so sick. But Beth is the one who insisted that I do it! She said she liked the smile on my face when I was coaching. She said, 'I never see you look happier than when you are out there on that football field.'"

Sounds familiar, doesn't it? Like Hannah McGee talking to Dad back in 1983.

Chapter 9

Hey Ref!

BEFORE WE HIT the stretch run of Dad's officiating career, it feels like a good time to take this project to the people.

As we (hopefully) have convinced you by now, growing up in a football officiating household teaches you so much about the game and the rules that govern that game. It also teaches you how to handle daily deluges of questions from friends, family, sports-loving strangers, or anyone who is curious about your father's life in stripes. Perhaps that's why Sam and I grew up to become a lawyer and a sportswriter, both of us asking other people questions for a living.

And while we have (hopefully) helped you achieve a better understanding of the what, how, and why of a college football official's career, we want to (hopefully) make sure we hit as many of the usual officiating questions that we can.

In the years following Dad's retirement from the field, I wrote a regular column for ESPN.com titled HEY REF! where readers could send in questions they had about his career, his thoughts on current officiating issues, and even what he thought about calls made in big games those very weeks.

As we were finishing up this book, one night I posted a tweet in the old "Hey Ref!" spirit, saying that it was now or never if anyone had any questions for Dr. Jerry McGee about his whistle blowing days. We received hundreds of replies. I boiled them down to a list of the most popular questions as well as some topics we haven't already hit. I also threw out all of the "What's it like to be blind?" and "Why do you hate my team?" comments.

I took the final list to Dad, and this is what he had to say.

"Who was the best player you shared the field with?"
Dad

When Julius Peppers was playing defensive end at North Carolina, it just wasn't fair. I never saw an athlete dominate an entire playing field like he did. And he played a little basketball, too.

On offense, Bo Jackson at Auburn. He was just on a different level than anyone else. Bo was the guy who walked out there and the entire stadium followed everything he did and everywhere he went, whether they were rooting for Auburn or not. Rocket Ismail at Notre Dame was like that, too. In the 1990 Orange Bowl he scored on a reverse and I have never seen anyone turn the corner and change gears like he did. He just blew right by everyone, including me.

But I also have to break it down into categories. I was with the wide receivers and defensive backs most of the time. Calvin Johnson at Georgia Tech and Herman Moore at Virginia were amazing at wide receiver. At DB, Dre Bly at North Carolina, Donnell Woolford at Clemson, and Deion Sanders at Florida State. And I have always said that if there was one minute remaining in the game and you could give me any quarterback to hand the ball and say, "We have to win this game," that would be Charlie Ward from Florida State. He was the best I ever shared a field with at moving his team down the field.

"Who was the fastest player you ever saw?"
Dad

We had a game at West Virginia in 1992, and the Mountaineers had the ball deep in their own territory. I think they were at the 22-yard line, so I was out at around 45. At the snap, this little wide receiver came downfield, right at me. I immediately started backing up. I was moving pretty good and had a big head start. By now I was on the other half of the field, at the 40, and he caught it at the 45, right in front of me. I was running as hard as I could run, but when he hit the goal line, I was way back at the 18. I had been beaten before, by five yards or something, but I felt like an idiot signaling touchdown running along nearly 20 yards behind the guy. He ran 45 yards in the time it took me to run 20.

Walking back up the sideline, I asked West Virginia head coach Don Nehlen, "Who the hell is that guy?"

He said, "That's James Jett. He just won a gold medal at the Barcelona Olympics three months ago."

"What are the worst field conditions and worst weather you ever had to deal with?"
Dad

In 2002, we had a big nationally televised Thursday night game, Florida State at Louisville, and Tropical Storm Isidore just sat on the stadium all night. But the field was amazing. The game went into overtime and it was the biggest win Louisville had ever had to that point. I remember the kid who scored the winning touchdown splashing around in a huge mud puddle in the end zone.

A few weeks later, we were at Charleston Southern in the rain and that field was not amazing. The water started pooling up all over the place. It was so bad that in some spots you couldn't see the sideline at all. The line would disappear into the water and come out again way downfield, so you would have to connect the dots as to where you thought the out-of-bounds line was. We had a punt that was rolling toward the end zone, but then it landed in a giant pool of water just short of the goal line and splashed to a stop. We were about to whistle the ball dead, but Virgil Valdez said, "Wait! It might float into the end zone!" When the game was over my white pants were so brown with mud that I just threw them away and left.

But the worst field conditions ever were at Penn State, of all places. It was Rutgers at Penn State and they had just installed a brand-new field, but there had been a ton of rain and the roots of the sod never took hold. It was like being on bad shag carpet. Every time you would try to make a turn and set your foot, it would buckle underneath you, coming up in sections of five or six feet at the time. The poor linemen couldn't block. They couldn't get traction. Every timeout a bunch of guys from the grounds crew would run out there with these poles and try to tamp it down. The next morning, my ankles have never been that sore. And this is a legendary agriculture school!

Sam

Let's not forget that Duke-Rutgers game at the Meadowlands in '87. Imagine all of that rain from Louisville or Charleston Southern, but then imagine it's about 30 degrees colder. It was raining so hard that it was coming into the tops of everyone's shoes, like someone was pouring ice water over your feet. The craziest part was that the fans left the seats and all stood under the lip of the upper deck, so you couldn't see them. Something would happen in the game and a cheer would go up, but the stadium looked empty. It was so weird.

Dad and the crew kept trying to fill out their penalty cards, but it was raining so hard the paper would just fall apart. So, they grab me and tell me I'm going to have to fill it out for them. At first, I would just write blind under my poncho. Ultimately, I ended up standing in the tunnel. There would be a penalty and I would run out there and one of the officials would shout over, "Holding on No. 78!" and I would run back up in the tunnel to write it down.

I turned 14 that week. I know people were like, "Why are the referees yelling stuff to that kid and why is he writing it down? Is he working on a school paper or something?"

Dad

The New York Giants had a game there the next day, and the CBS Sports TV guys were staying at our hotel. Before the game we were all dressed in the lobby ready to leave, and we heard this guy laughing at us. "You have to go referee a game out there in *this?!*" He couldn't stop laughing. It was John Madden.

"What did you do when you had to go to the bathroom during a game?"
Dad

I never had an issue with that. But one day, one of my crewmates did. It was a small college game back in the 1970s, I don't even remember where, but we had a guy back then who was notorious for going out the night before games. In our pregame meeting he looked terrible, clearly hungover. He said to us, "Boys, I'm not sure I can go out there today." But we told him he had to. We weren't going to work the game with four guys.

Late in the first half, he was kind of gripping his stomach. He looked green. He was in a bad way. During a timeout he said to us, "Man, I really have to get to halftime so I can get to the bathroom." But there were a couple of timeouts and a couple of penalties and it took forever. He kept looking at the clock like, *Dammit, I'm not going to make it.*

Finally, with time still on the clock, he tells us he can't wait and he heads for the locker room, walking straight down the middle of the field, all by himself. The crowd sees him. He started walking a little more briskly, a little bowlegged, and the fans realize what's happening. This ref needs to get to the toilet. The walk turns into a jog. The crowd starts cheering. The jog turns into an all-out sprint and now the crowd is going nuts. He's going to make it!

Then, all of the sudden, he just stops, like right at the goal line, and freezes. It's too late. He's going. Now the crowd can't decide if they should cheer, laugh, or boo.

He did not officiate the second half with us. When the game was over, he was long gone.

"What's the biggest regular season game you ever officiated?"
Dad

I still think maybe the biggest regular season game in the history of the ACC was Georgia Tech at Virginia, November 3, 1990. Virginia was ranked No. 1 for the first time ever. Georgia Tech was ranked 16th. You had Shawn Moore throwing to Herman Moore for Virginia, and both of those guys were being mentioned as Heisman candidates. I was in the defensive backfield with Ken Swilling from Georgia Tech, who was one of the greatest defensive players I've ever seen. Tech kicked a field goal with seven seconds remaining to win 41–38 and then went on to win a share of the national championship. I've never been in a stadium with more energy than that one.

But what I remember most about that day was that we were in the locker room, having our pregame meeting, and we'd already had a really intense meeting the night before. We were all totally focused. Then one of the guys from Virginia came in and said, "Well, great news, guys. It looks like we won't have to cancel the game."

Won't have to cancel the game? What the hell was he talking about?

The night before, someone had broken into Scott Stadium and set the field on fire. They had scorched a whole section of the Astroturf at the 50-yard line and the grounds crew scrambled to cut out that section and stitched it up with some spare turf they had stored at the baseball stadium.

We had been so focused on our pregame Friday night and Saturday morning, we had no idea.

Sam

Virginia still had a chance to be a top-five team, but quarterback Shawn Moore injured his passing hand two weeks later against Maryland and they lost again. People all over the country, and friends at my school, were like, "He must have hurt his hand when it hit someone during the game." I would say, no, he hurt when was mad about a play and he slammed his fist on that artificial turf. They would go, "Yeah, well, how do *you* know that?" I said because I was standing on the sideline, like 20 feet from him, when he did it!

"What's the craziest game you ever officiated?"
Dad

Navy at North Texas, November 10, 2007. Navy won 74–62 and there was no overtime. It set the FBS record for points scored in a regulation game, and that record stood for nearly a decade. We knew it was going to be crazy because Navy was ranked last in the nation in passing defense and North Texas was ranked first in passing offense, but Navy was ranked first in the nation in rushing offense and North Texas was ranked second-to-last in the nation in rushing defense.

They basically played an entire football game in just the second quarter. We had 10 kickoffs in that quarter. Ten! The score in that quarter alone was 35–28. A North Texas receiver had five touchdown catches in one game. After a while, it was so ridiculous we were just laughing as we ran down the sideline. I was on the North Texas sideline and they kept yelling, "Keep going, Doc!" Then the turning point of the game was, of all things, a safety. Navy took a two-point lead on a safety, North Texas kicked off, and Navy ran that kick back for a touchdown.

The night before the game we had eaten dinner at a great steakhouse. We said, "Man, after the game tomorrow night we're coming back here and having a nice meal." But we were so exhausted we were all laid up at the hotel with beer and pizza, icing our knees and ankles.

"What's the best quote you ever heard from a player?"
Dad

In the early 1980s, Clemson had a wide receiver named Keith Jennings. His brother was Stanford Jennings, who played in the NFL forever with the Bengals. Keith was huge, like

6-foot-4, 230 pounds. One day at NC State, like on the first play of the game, he caught a pass and a defensive back had the play read perfectly, but Jennings just lowered his shoulder and completely ran through the guy. It was like he had tackled the guy instead of the other way around. After the play, Jennings helped the guy up, and as he did, he said to him, "I'm pretty good, ain't I?"

"What's the best prank you ever pulled or saw pulled?"
Dad

Terry Monk is an all-timer as a referee. He was the white hat with us in the '97 Rose Bowl. One year he worked the Independence Bowl, when it was the Poulan Weed Eater Independence Bowl (the greatest bowl sponsor name there's ever been).

They had a room set up at the hotel in Shreveport for the officials where they could meet and hang out, and Poulan had decorated it with Weed Eater boxes. They were empty boxes, just for display. One of the officials came in late, so Terry and those guys decided to punish him for it. When he got there, they all told him that when they checked in, they had all gotten free Weed Eaters. He was mad. He hadn't gotten one! Even on the field right after the coin toss, Terry said, "Does anyone have anything to say before we kick this off?" And the guy was pouting. "Yeah, I still haven't gotten my damn Weed Eater."

The next day, there's a box waiting for him at checkout. It's a Poulan Weed Eater box. He was so excited, but the box was big and heavy. He put his family in one cab to the airport and he had to get another cab just for himself and this box. He paid extra to check it on the plane, but whatever, he was really excited.

He got home and when opened it up, the box was just jammed full of trash. They had taken one of those display boxes, filled it up with whatever they could find in the room, and taped it up.

So, young officials out there, what's the lesson? Don't be late.

"What's the best conversation you had with a player during a game?"
Dad

My favorite was actually right before a game. That 1990 Orange Bowl just felt so gigantic. National championship on the line, a couple dozen future NFL players in the game. I remember we were sitting in the locker room and a voice said, "Have a great game, guys!" It was O.J. Simpson, who was a sideline reporter for NBC that night. Franco Harris and Bill Walsh stopped to wish us luck, too.

I got the captains from Notre Dame for the coin toss and one of them was the quarterback, Tony Rice. He was a little nervous, and so was I. As we walked out of the tunnel onto the field, I said to him, "Where you from, Rice?" I already knew the answer. He told me he was a little town in Upstate South Carolina called Woodruff. I told him that I lived near there, that I worked at Furman University and that my sons went to a rival school to his, Travelers Rest High School.

"Tony Rice, what in the world is a guy from Woodruff, South Carolina, and a guy from Travelers Rest doing here, walking onto the field at the Orange Bowl?"

We laughed all the way to the 50-yard line.

"Who was the most famous person you met on the sideline?"
Dad

I used to love keeping my eye out to see who was on the sidelines. At Miami there were always a ton of former great players hanging around. Jim Kelly, Bernie Kosar, Vinnie Testeverde, Michael Irvin, whichever NFL guys had the weekend off, it seemed like they were always on the sideline at Miami. Burt Reynolds, who played at Florida State and lived in Tallahassee, was always at FSU and always giving us grief, but in a joking way. Adam Sandler and all of those guys, when they were working on the *The Longest Yard* remake with Burt, they were around. At Temple, Bill Cosby used to reach out and steal our penalty flags. Someone would reach for their flag off their belt and it wouldn't be there. He'd be on the sideline, holding it in his hand.

But I've never seen anyone more excited to be at a college football game than George Lucas, of *Star Wars* fame. He was grand marshal of the Rose Parade in 2007 and when it was time for the coin toss, here he came, marching out to midfield, saying, "Isn't this great?!" He had Darth Vader with him and everything.

Ryan

I am a *Star Wars* nut. Never before had I been jealous of Dad's football experiences, but that day I was. I was watching on TV at home 3,000 miles from Pasadena, and could see Dad and the crew chatting it up with Lucas and Vader. The phone rang. It was my best friend from high school. He said, "Finally, we have verification of what we've always known. The refs are totally from the Dark Side of the Force."

"Why did you never move up to the NFL?"
Dad

I never wanted to. The way you ask that question is the same way most people ask it, but it's not accurate. To me, and to a lot of us, the NFL wasn't a move up. We loved college football. Now, I had a lot of colleagues who moved on to the NFL, and that's what they wanted to do—especially when I was in the Big East, where so many of those guys had grown up in the northeast, where the NFL was always king. And I have loved watching so many of my friends working the NFL postseason and Super Bowls.

There were windows when I could have done it. But I also had my day jobs, which were taking up more and more time, and Hannah and the boys. Every NFL weekend is multiple nights, there is frequent cross-country travel, and with preseason games, the season lasts so long.

I have so much admiration for NFL officials, but they are not necessarily the best refs in the country. They are the best of those who wanted to be in the NFL.

The NFL is the dream for a lot of officials. It was never mine.

"Who was the craziest fan you ever had to deal with?"
Dad

We'd had a very clean game at South Carolina. No controversial calls. Big difference in the score. Zero issues. None. As soon as the game was over, we were hustled into a van at Williams-Brice Stadium, still in in uniform, and we're trying to back out and we can't leave.

There was one woman who was standing behind the van, slapping the window with one hand and just screaming at us. *"You damned cheating SOBs!"* Just over and over, screaming at us. She was so skinny, she looked like a skeleton, and she had a cigarette hanging off her lip, barely hanging on. And in the hand that she wasn't using to smack the van, she was holding a baby.

*"What's the craziest thing anyone ever threw
onto the field?"*
Dad

Thankfully, this didn't happen much. I was always a little worried about that. But we were so far away from the stands, it wasn't usually a problem. There was one time we had an official who had to leave a game because he was hit by a coin that someone had thrown from the stands and it hit him in the calf. That might not sound like much, but if someone has fired that thing from the upper deck and it hits you, that's really dangerous. We had a guy hit with a liquor bottle at Georgia Tech.

But as for crazy, the only time someone topped the high school chain crew who threw all their markers onto the field over my head, it was from the student section at Boston College. There was a routine incomplete pass play, no contact or anything, and a penalty flag came sailing over my head and landed right on the exact spot where the play had happened. Referee Walter Davenport came over. "Jerry, what you got?" I said, "Walter, I don't have a damn thing. That flag came in from the stands."

Walter got on the microphone and warned the crowd about throwing objects onto the field, but the Boston College coaches and I couldn't stop laughing about it. I walked over in front of the student section and I held both flags in my hands, looking at one and then the other. Then I just shrugged and stuck them both in my pockets. The students thought that was pretty funny.

*"What was the one play that made you say,
'I can't believe that just happened!'"*
Dad

I wish I could remember who the player was, but it was a defensive back at Pitt. The wide receiver and this defender were across the field. In my earliest days in the ACC, Mr. Neve had always taught us that you look through your play so you can anticipate what's happening. So, I was watching my guys downfield, but I was also looking at the quarterback and saw he was going to throw it deep down the other sideline.

That DB had it played perfectly, had great inside position. He went to intercept the pass, but I immediately thought, *Well, he jumped too soon.* He had timed it wrong. But hell, he stayed in the air. Like, hung there, and he intercepted the ball. I thought, *Did I really see what I think I saw?*

The side judge was Tommy Tomczak, and at halftime he pulled me into the showers away from the other guys and asked, "Did you get a good look at that interception?" I told him yes, and he said, "That damn kid stayed in the air! He jumped too soon, but he just hung up there until the ball got there." I told him that was exactly what I thought. We both were so relieved someone else saw it because we realized we weren't crazy.

But we also agreed that maybe we should keep that to ourselves.

"What's the biggest misperception about college football officials?"
Dad

That we just show up and officiate a game and then leave, and that we show up for money and fame.

No one knows about all the work that went into the preparation for that game. Rules clinics and local meetings and film study and rules exams and scrimmages and physical conditioning, all of that. One year before a season opener I did the math. Before the first ball had been placed on a tee, I had already worked 300 hours that year on officiating. By season's end, what I was paid versus how much I'd worked came to about 12 cents per hour.

"Did any big power broker, like a conference commissioner, ever try to influence how you called a game?"
Dad

Never. Not even close. Now, there were administrators who would be on the sideline and weren't happy with a call. During my small college days, we were at Mars Hill College one day and they were hosting Liberty University—I guess they were Liberty Baptist College then. At one point, Dr. Jerry Falwell was all the way out on the field, screaming, *"Do you work for Mars Hill?!"*

But we never saw the conference commissioners anywhere other than the rules clinic. And even then, it was just to stop by and check in. People forget officials are not employees of the conference. They are independent contractors who are assigned games by the conference.

Gene Corrigan, who was commissioner of the ACC during most of my first stint in the conference, we would only see at the clinic. But he wouldn't have input on how we officiated. He would help make decisions about uniforms or something like that. Like the year he said we were no longer wearing shorts.

"Wait…you wore shorts?!"
Dad

Yes. Those were only in the ACC and only for a couple of seasons in the 1980s. I think I wore them in only five or six games. The idea was that it was so hot in the Southeast in August and September, they would be cooler. But they were those heavy polyester coaches' shorts, and we had socks pulled up over our calves, so there was nothing cool about it.

Ryan

They certainly didn't look cool, especially on the chunkier officials. I have one photo of Dad in his shorts, standing with Doug Rhoads on the field prior to a game at Duke. Rhoads threatened to send his old FBI coworkers to my house if I ever published it on ESPN.com.

Dad

Mr. Neve was like a drill sergeant about a lot of things, but especially when it came to uniforms. We weren't allowed to wear long sleeves because he liked how short sleeves looked. The white hats would plead with him to wear long sleeves when we worked games at Maryland late in the season. We even had a crew in the Amos Alonzo Stagg Bowl, the NCAA Division III championship, played in Atlantic City, New Jersey, in December. It was cold, and they begged him to not wear short sleeves. He told them he appreciated them calling and that he could send a replacement crew if they didn't want to wear the short sleeves. They stopped complaining. But it was 20 degrees at kickoff.

At one of my earliest ACC rules clinics, Mr. Neve had us dress in our uniforms and stand out in the motel parking lot, lined up for inspection like I'd had to do in the Army National Guard. "You need new shoes…Your belt is the wrong color… You need a new hat…"

While we were out there, a door to one of the rooms opened up. It was Bones McKinney, the legendary Wake Forest basketball coach, in the same town where we were for a speaking engagement. He came out of the door, froze, went back into his room, and peeked at us through the curtains. Then he finally came back out and said, "Thank goodness it's just you guys. I saw all these referees out here and I thought I had died and gone to hell."

And finally, the question that was asked the most. Like, dozens of times. Drumroll, please...

> *"What's the one call you wish you*
> *could have another look at?*
> **Ryan**

Okay, I'll take this one because I know the answer. So does Sam, and so should you, by now. Yes, it's that second quarter touchdown in the '85 Citrus Bowl, the play Dad still insists he got wrong and Sam and I still believe he got right.

David Miles was the BYU receiver who caught that pass. While working on this book, I found Miles in Salt Lake City, working as the director of event and support services at the headquarters of the Church of Jesus Christ of Latter-Day Saints. On December 28, 1985, he was a reserve sophomore receiver who hadn't expected to see the field against the Buckeyes, let alone catch a touchdown pass.

When I got him on the phone, Miles told me that just the day before he'd been talking smack about that catch when an Ohio State loyalist coworker had brought up the game. He also told me that the mouse pad on his desk is a black-and-white photo of him celebrating the score in Orlando, his arms raised in celebration next to Dad, whose arms are also in the air, signaling touchdown, and that led to telling me about all of the joy that moment has brought to his life for more than three and a half decades, even in a loss.

When Miles was sent into the game late in the second quarter, his only job was to run a decoy route down the middle while the real pass play was run to the far side of the field. "I was half-jogging, to be honest," Miles recalled. "I saw Robbie Bosco planting his foot to throw, but he was looking away from Mark Bellini, our No. 1 receiver who was supposed to get the ball on that play. I realized something was wrong and the ball was in the air, so I pivoted and really started running downfield to get under it.

"When I caught the ball around the 8-yard line and turned toward the end zone, the defender was right behind me and we ran right at your dad. All I was thinking was, 'Get the ball inside that front corner pylon…get that ball inside the front corner pylon…'"

For 35 years we have known that David Miles did get that ball inside the front corner pylon. But what we haven't known is whether or not his right foot stepped out of bounds before the ball broke the plane as he planted to leap toward paydirt.

Who was right? Dad, saying he missed the call, or Sam and me, saying that he was right? The answer was finally going to be revealed!

"Your Dad is right; my right foot was on the line," Miles said. "But I have said ever since that day that the official on that play, your dad, had no chance to see it clearly. The defender was diving for me as I was diving for the end zone, and his head was completely blocking the view of my foot.

"Thank goodness we didn't have replay then, because if we had, I think they would have taken my touchdown away and we would have it at the 1-yard line. But we didn't have replay, and there were only a handful of TV cameras there that day. He made the best call he could in the time that it happened. He trusted that I got into the end zone, because that's what he had to work with that day."

Sensing he might have crushed my 14-year-old soul, David Miles had a message for the man whom until now he'd known only as "the ref on my touchdown." Now the guy on his mousepad has a name: Dr. Jerry McGee of North Carolina.

"I scored a touchdown because your father said I did. That makes it official. That's my story and I'm sticking to it. In 1985, I was a really big deal because of it. And in 2020, I'm still having fun with it. So, if that's his one big missed call that's been bugging him all these years, maybe it will help him to know that he has helped make my life a lot more enjoyable during all those same years.

"You tell your dad he was a great college football official. And I'm really glad he was officiating on that play."

Sam (still defiant)

I still think the hand with the ball might have crossed the goal line before he planted his foot.

Dad (laughing)

Okay, so I only got 64,479 of 64,480 plays right.

Family Timeout
with Danny Caddell

"I had kind of gotten used to crappy referee's tickets, so on this day I figured there had to have been a mistake. We were damn near on the bench!"

It is Christmas 2019, and Uncle Danny has me rolling. We've been talking about this book, and about our trip together to Dad's final game a decade earlier. He laughs when he recalls the first big UNC–Clemson game in '83, when he caught Dad throwing up a prayer to the football gods while the Tar Heels kept throwing Hail Marys in his direction. Danny hadn't heard the "it's a sad frog who can't pull for his own pond" quote gifted to me and Sam by his father in the skybox at Death Valley. He reminds me their mother, Mary Caddell, also known as Ma-Ma, attended a few games as well, and when he does, I suddenly remember that she sat with me for the first-ever night game at Duke's Wallace Wade Stadium, a win over Indiana in a 1984.

We are having a good time.

But not as good of a time as Danny had one Saturday evening in Tallahassee, having traveled to the Florida Panhandle from Eastern North Carolina with his best friend to see Dad officiate in one of the sport's greatest rivalries, Miami versus Florida State. Over Christmas ham, he tells me the story.

"We were on the front row, right on the 50-yard line. I mean, we're so close I wouldn't have been surprised if one of the teams had said, 'Here's a jersey, y'all just come on down here with us.'"

Uncle Danny remembers Dad walking out for the pregame warmups, in uniform, and coming straight to them with a couple of game programs that had been left in the officials' locker room. Soon, the FSU fans were staring, wondering what in the world a ref was doing talking to these guys.

"Your daddy realized that we were drawing a crowd. He says, really loud so that they can all hear him, 'Hey, Danny, did you bring your glasses?!' I said, 'No, man, I don't believe I brought them with me...'"

According to Danny, Dad threw his hands up.

"He said, 'Well, I don't know what I'm going to do! I don't have mine, either! You know I can't see a damn thing without my glasses!' He shook our hands like, 'Oh well, I'll do my best...' and went onto the field. Now these Florida State people are all like, wait a minute, what the hell is going on here?

"We just waved and shouted to him, 'Have a great game!'"

CHAPTER 10

CHANGING
OF THE GUARD
AND OF THE GAME

T HE EARLY 2000S was a time of uneasiness for our
family, still trying to find our footing after the loss of
Mom. But it was also a complicated time for everyone, and
the college football world was certainly no exception. By 2004,
another sea change of conference realignment was rolling.
Miami and Virginia Tech followed Dad, leaving the Big East
for the ACC. Boston College soon followed.

The entire world became unmoored on 9/11, when hijacked
aircraft were steered into the World Trade Center, rural Penn-
sylvania, and the Pentagon. Among the very first responders to
the Pentagon attack was Northern Virginia firefighter and ACC
back judge Pat Ryan. Another ACC official, Colonel Timon
Oujiri, was working in the Pentagon at the time of the attack.

Dad

Our first game back after 9/11 was Maryland at Wake Forest, and from that day forward, our routine changed forever.

The most sobering moment for me was when we were in the locker room getting dressed, like I had hundreds of times, but this time a security team came into the room. They said, "Okay, let's go over some procedures here in case there is a bomb…"

The reality of hearing that was hard to believe. "If there is a terrorist attack on the stadium, we will come to you and get you off the field and we will take you to a predetermined location until we get the all clear."

I was at that game. It's odd to think back now on how unusual it felt because in the years since we have all become so used to standing in line to have our bags and bodies searched. But that day, seeing those long lines at every gate of Groves Stadium, was unsettling. I was on the sideline, and even with 25,000 people there, watching a good one-score game, it was the quietest football field I've ever been on. Everyone, including Dad, his crew, and the two teams, had arrived assuming it would simply be another fall Saturday, a chance to return to normalcy. But reality settled in after kickoff. There was a new normal.

Ever since that season, officials take part in what's called the "110 Minute Meeting," a gathering of stadium, team, game, and security officials to go over any safety concerns.

Dad

One of the questions that people have always asked is if I ever felt unsafe officiating football games. For nearly 40 years, my answer to that was that I'd only felt uneasy at a handful of high school games, where some rough guys might have stalked me during the game, and then I had to walk to my car alone in some small town somewhere.

Even after seeing an official hit by a liquor bottle thrown from the stands at Georgia Tech and having tires slashed in our hotel parking lot in Charlottesville, the only time I felt uneasy was during those days after 9/11 and then the very next year. We had a game at Maryland right in the middle of that awful time when the Washington D.C. sniper had the whole city fearing for their safety. There were two guys shooting people at random all over the area for three weeks.

When we went to rent cars at the hotel, we were running zig-zags and hiding behind other cars. Everyone in the city was. We got to the stadium and it's time for us to take up our spots during pregame warmups, an hour before the game. All we can think is, *We're going to be out there in striped shirts in a stadium that's open on one end. We're perfect targets.* So, we wore our black jackets. We really were nervous about the whole thing.

In the middle of such a terrifying atmosphere, they grabbed levity wherever they could get it. ACC officiating coordinator Tommy Hunt decided to make a surprise visit to show support for the crew placed into such a stressful situation. Like any other job, the staff tends to act a little differently when the boss is around. So, when Dad was walking out of the locker room and saw Hunt about to walk in, he greeted him extra loudly to send a heads-up back to the crew. "WELL, HEY TOMMY. WHAT A NICE SURPRISE."

From the locker room, the shouts came back, "Yeah, okay, f--k you, McGee! F--king Tommy Hunt wouldn't come up here into this f--king mess!" just as the boss strolled in.

The 2000s also brought a swelling of the bowl calendar. In 1990, there were 18 bowl games. In 2001, that number was up to 25. By the end of the decade it was 35. The good news is that meant more opportunities for an official to spend their holidays working one more game. The bad news was that with new games popping up and disappearing like a Whack-a-Mole game, they no had no idea where those bowl assignments might be.

In 2000, Dad worked the Motor City Bowl in Detroit between Marshall and Cincinnati in the Pontiac Silverdome. On Christmas Day 2001, it was USC versus Utah in the Sega Las Vegas Bowl. The next year brought Southern Miss and Oklahoma State in the Houston Bowl.

Dad

The best part of that Vegas Bowl was before the game. We'd had our pregame meeting and we'd gotten dressed and were waiting to go out, and there was a knock on the locker room door. It was a pair of Vegas showgirls. "Do you guys mind if we get dressed in here?" We said, *No ma'am, not at all.*

Say what you want about the Vegas Bowl, but that never happened at the Fiesta or the Rose.

It wasn't that Dad wasn't having as much fun as he'd had in years past; it's that it felt like no one was having as much fun as in years past. Instant replay was in its infancy. So was social media. Both tools could be a college football official's best friend and worst enemy all at once. Film had become video, video had become digital, and high-definition video became the standard. Now, film study, previously limited to Friday pregame and offseason rules meetings, was landing in email inboxes all the time. For college officials who were working their day jobs during the week, their part-time gig was starting to feel like a poorly paying second full-time gig.

Speaking of money, the college football arms race was moving into a rate of speed that no one could have foreseen. Dad was a firsthand witness to the ushering in of this new era, serving on multiple NCAA committees, most notably as the representative of Division II schools on the NCAA Presidents Council, in the room with the leaders of the FBS institutions that were steering the sport he officiated into uncharted financial territory.

Dad

It was a front row seat to seeing where Notre Dame and Ohio State and schools like that, with so much football money to make and spend, were going to take the sport, whether the others could keep up or not.

The benefit of that spending spree was that the officials' Saturday places of work were being transformed into football palaces. But more money spent on facilities and coaches meant that universities and their alums would demand more wins more quickly in order to justify their generosity. The pressure of expectation started tightening the collars of those coaches' new designer suits. So they started pushing on the officials more. And the officials started pushing back.

Dad

There were still good guys and bad guys. That never changed. But it certainly started becoming more adversarial.

Sam

I think for Dad, too, there just weren't as many of the old guard around. They were starting to hang it up. Dad and Booker had also been separated after 10 seasons together. Part of the problem there was missing your best friend, but it was also getting used to someone else on your side of the field. There's a trust there that has to be built, and it doesn't happen immediately.

That being said, the veteran guys who were around and on Dad's crew, they kind of all took on this "we aren't taking any bull from anyone" attitude. And I mean, they really stopped taking it.

One day at Clemson, Tommy Bowden was really jawing at Dad about something, and Dad looked at him and said, "You know, Tommy, you look cute when you're mad." Bowden just stopped and looked at Dad like, *What did he just say?* So, it worked!

One Saturday afternoon an ACC crew in South Bend, Indiana, for a Navy–Notre Dame contest received a surprise visit from Fighting Irish head coach Bob Davie. The coach, already on the hot seat, walked into the locker room and said, "ACC officials, huh? Well, you better be ready. This is isn't f--king Duke versus Wake Forest!"

Referee Jim Knight looked up from lacing his shoes and said, "Yeah, well it isn't Miami–Florida State either, Coach. That's where we were last week."

Sam

My favorite Jimmy Knight story was at Navy. There had been some lightning, and when that happens there is a mandatory delay. The officials were in the locker room waiting out the delay when a Naval Academy staffer came in and said "The Commandant says it is time to start the game." Jimmy smiled and said, "You tell the Commandant that I have a bronze star and a Purple Heart from Vietnam. I'm not getting any medals today."

A little while later, the kid came back and said, "The Commandant says we will start when you are ready to start."

The ACC Old Timers crew never lacked for character. Some were already retired by the 2000s, but others were still out there grinding. "Those are the guys I like to see walk out onto the football field for one of my games," Wake Forest head coach Jim Grobe told me in a 2009 interview for *ESPN The Magazine*. "I am all about training up young guys, but I feel a lot better when I see guys out there that have grey hair and crow's feet. I want some experience calling my games."

Knight, an ACC official since 1974, had frightened the sports world in 1997 after suffering an in-game heart attack at a Virginia–UNC game live on ABC, but came back to work several more years. Clark Gaston, who'd worked with Dad since the 1970s, kept going until 2006, despite knees creakier than a pirate ship run aground. When another Clemson lineman-turned-ACC official, Mark Kane, had suffered a heart attack but came back later in the same season, it was Gaston who greeted him by emptying the giant bag of footballs. You know, in case they needed something to carry Kane home in.

Dad

We had a guy named Bob Cooper, a referee, and he was tough as granite, but I still smile every single time I hear his name. Bob never got stressed out over much. He was almost too loose. He's the one who left me hanging on that punt spot in my very first ACC game.

One day, there was a marching band sitting right behind the end zone, and they kept playing every time the opposing team tried to call a play. Doing it on purpose to disrupt them. We warned them and the public address guy even told them to stop. They didn't stop. So, Bob ran all the way down the middle of the field, 60 or 70 yards, to that end zone. He went into a pose and started conducting the band, flailing his arms. Then he jerked them apart, boom, like an orchestra conductor would at the end of a big number.

They stopped and the band members roared in laughter. He ran back up the field and they never played again when they weren't supposed to. He never said a word.

All you need to know about Bob Cooper is that during the very brief phase of ACC officials wearing shorts, he lobbied, albeit unsuccessfully, to have his crew wear their short pants for a chilly midseason game at Army, for no reason other than he wanted to see how the uniform-obsessed West Point crowd would react.

During a televised North Carolina–Wake Forest game, Cooper turned on his microphone, faced the cameras, and announced, "We have a false start on the offense…" and pointed the wrong way, toward the defense. Dad shouted, "Bob! Other way! Other way!" So, Cooper took his hand, wiped the air in circles as if the world was his school room chalkboard, erasing what he'd just said and done, and started his announcement over.

Sam

I was with Dad and Booker at Clemson. Cooper had been assigned to the game, but he'd never booked a motel room. So, he just shows up and says, "I'm going to say with you guys." There was no room, but we got a rollaway bed and stuck it in the corner. Later that night we were all ready for bed and we couldn't find Cooper. He was still in the hotel bar.

Booker says, 'Y'all help me get this bed out of here..." and we proceeded to roll it outside on the sidewalk, right outside our door. We put his bags on it and everything.

We waited for him to see it and bang on the door all mad, but it never happened. So, we went to sleep. The next morning, we looked outside, and there was Cooper, in the bed, asleep, on the sidewalk.

With the old guard on the way out, Dad started wondering if perhaps he should start thinking about following them. Now he had grandbabies. In November 2004, Erica and I had our daughter, Tara, two days after Dad had worked Virginia at Georgia Tech. Sam and Marci had their first, Hannah Cole, less than two months later, with little brother, Brooks, soon to follow.

Dad was also about to meet the woman who would become our stepmother, Marcella McInnis, who came from a long line of UNC Tar Heels, but thankfully held no grudges about the onside kick in the '83 Maryland game. After a decade as president at Wingate University, he had everything in overdrive. The school had grown from 1,000 students to 3,200, and there were construction cranes all over campus, building 37 new buildings. He'd added a dozen graduate programs. The school had become one of the national leaders in producing

Academic All-Americans. He had 540 employees and a $100 million annual budget.

In other words, there were a lot of reasons to hang up his striped jersey.

Dad

Once the three Big East schools moved to the ACC and the conference went to 12 members, we all knew that the inaugural ACC Championship Game was coming in 2005. I told the boys that if I got that game, that would be it.

Sam

It felt like it was the perfect plan. I couldn't think of a better way to go out. He had always joked that if he got the Rose Bowl again, maybe he would break on a ball, pick it off, run it back for a touchdown, and take off up the tunnel, never to be seen again. We would joke about what he would say when David Letterman had him on his show the next night.

But he had already done the Rose Bowl and so many huge games. This game was going to be brand-new. No one had done this one, and only one group would ever be the guys who did the first one.

He did get it. The 22nd-ranked Florida State Seminoles versus No. 5 Virginia Tech. A rematch of the classic 2000 national title game that was won by FSU but made Virginia Tech quarterback Michael Vick a college football legend. A win for the Hokies, led by Vick's little brother, Marcus, would send them to the BCS National Championship Game.

It was indeed the perfect plan. So, Sam and I booked our travel for Jacksonville, cashing in vacation days and leaving our wives at home alone with two little babies. But we weren't missing this. The atmosphere was every bit as electric as the big bowl games we had attended together in our younger days.

Sam

Ryan and I were both so busy and both had little girls at home, and I don't think I realized how long it had been since we'd been together like that for one of Dad's games. I think we both had been at games separately, but not together. The seats were great. We laughed a lot. It was a lot of fun. And it ended up being a good football game.

That part was a surprise. Virginia Tech, favored by two touchdowns, was nervous and sloppy, and FSU jumped out to a big lead. But then Vick led the Hokies back to within five points and his team had the ball in the closing minutes.

You've read plenty about the perks of being in an official's family, but now you will learn about perhaps the biggest problem. If you arrived to the game with the officials, then you also have to be ready to leave the game with the officials. If they have chosen to get dressed at the hotel instead of the stadium at a big postseason game, then that also means they will be sprinting off the field and into a waiting van to be whisked away via police escort and taken back to the hotel in a matter of minutes.

That's all fine and good if the game is a blowout or, as is the case for many family members, you don't care about the game at all. But, as you have also read plenty about by now, not caring about the game was never the case for Ryan and Sam McGee.

Sam

At that 1990 Orange Bowl, Notre Dame is driving to put away the game and determine the national championship, and some guy walks up and says, "Sorry, time to go!" Ryan and I were so mad. We made the guy take us the long way around to the exit, still in the stadium, so we could keep watching the last big drive. Then we stood in the tunnel until the last possible second to see Notre Dame score, and then we ran to the van.

Mom finally said, "Boys, I know this a big deal. But it is not a big enough deal for us to have to walk back to the hotel."

Sam

Now, 15 years later, we were doing the exact same thing. We made the guy in charge of watching the families so mad. Virginia Tech scored and were down five with a little less than two minutes remaining. They were going to attempt an onside kick and Ryan and I were trying to watch from the tunnel and the old guy is yelling, "You have to get into the van!"

We didn't care. It's Dad's last game. What do we have to lose, right? So, we yell back, "No!"

The onside kick failed. Tech recovered, but it hadn't traveled quite 10 yards. What a ridiculously apropos symmetrical end to Dad's career, going back to his first huge call, the onside kick at Maryland that also determined an ACC championship.

Sam and I ran to the van, much to our handlers' relief. We listened to Florida State run out the clock on the van radio while the crowd that we could no longer see cheered all around us. Seconds after the game clock hit all zeroes, Dad came running off the field and jumped into the back seat of the van beside us. The police lights started flashing. The vans carrying the officials and their families peeled out of the Gator Bowl, snaked through the crowd that was now pouring out of the stadium gates, and we hammered down I-95 toward our hotel.

Sam and I leaned over, reached out to shake Dad's hand, and said, "Congratulations on an amazing career."

Dad's eyes stayed pointed straight ahead.

"I think I'll do one more year."

Coach's Timeout
with Bobby Bowden

"Your daddy worked so many of our dadgum games back then. But if I'm being totally honest with you, the first time I saw him I had him as the wrong Jerry McGee."

It is on or near National Signing Day in Tallahassee, Florida. I am in Tallahassee to cover the harvesting of another crazy-talented FSU recruiting class. Bobby Bowden is still being referred to as "the recently retired Florida State head coach," and I have stopped by an off-campus function where Seminoles fans have been promised face time with some Florida State football legends.

Bowden, winner of 377 games (389 if you still count those vacated by the NCAA), two national championships, a dozen ACC titles, and the father of fellow head coaches Tommy and Terry, is shaking hands and signing autographs. At his side is Mickey Andrews, his defensive coordinator of 24 years. They both retired from football in 2009, one year after Dad.

Dad officiated more than a dozen FSU games coached by Bowden and Andrews, including rivalry matchups at Florida and Miami, the so-called Bowden Bowl between Bobby Bowden's Seminoles and Tommy Bowden's Clemson Tigers, and an oppressively hot Labor Day weekend Kickoff Classic at the New Jersey Meadowlands against the Kansas Jayhawks.

Andrews was always one of Dad's sideline favorites. I find out on this night that the feeling is mutual.

"What I wanted to see was a lot of gray hair on my referees," Andrews explains. "If they didn't have any, I thought it was my job to give them some."

This had long been verified to me by Dad, who has always told the story of Andrews riding a young rookie ACC official during an early season FSU cupcake game. During a timeout,

Andrews approached the official with a very detailed rules question. When the youngster tripped over his explanation, Andrews cut him off. "Why did I even bother asking you? If you were worth a s--t and actually knew the rules you'd be working a real game today instead of this bulls--t."

"Yeah," Andrews says when I tell him that story, laughing. "That was a good one. I did that a few times."

But now we both turn to Coach Bowden to finish his story. The wrong Jerry McGee?

"Yeah, so we get the names of the officials working our game and I see 'Jerry McGee from the ACC.' I think, okay, I know who he is! But I really didn't."

Wait. I know where this is going. There is indeed another Jerry McGee. He and his twin brother, Mike, played football at Duke and both went on to great coaching and sport administration careers. Mike, who served as athletic director at both USCs—Southern California and South Carolina—was also head football coach at Duke, with Jerry as his defensive coordinator. The duo also did a stint at Dad's alma mater, East Carolina. Jerry went on to have a decorated career as a North Carolina high school sports administrator. This was all taking place during the 1970s and '80s, when my Jerry McGee was moving up the officiating and college administration ladders, and also in North Carolina.

Confused? Yeah, well, join the club. Remember Ed Emory, the high school coach who had Dad and his crew thrown out of a Wadesboro, North Carolina, steakhouse? He also went on to be head coach at East Carolina, and one day gave a tour of the football offices to our entire family, during which he introduced my father to everyone as Mike McGee. He did it so many times that even now, years later, I still call Dad "Mike." Adding to the confusion, in 2012 and 2015 the two Jerry McGees were inducted into the North Carolina Sports

Hall of Fame, my father first and the other Jerry McGee three years later. Mike McGee—the actual Mike McGee, not the Jerry McGee that Ed Emory thought was Mike McGee—had already entered that same Hall of Fame years earlier.

But it turns out the president of the Jerry McGee Confusion Club might very well have been Bobby Bowden.

"The referees come out there before the game and I am walking over to say hello and I said to the person I was with, 'Wait, which one of these guys is Jerry McGee?' And he points to the field judge and says, 'There he is, Coach.' Now, Ryan, your daddy isn't a big guy, is he?"

No, Coach, he's not.

"I thought, 'Oh my goodness, poor Jerry McGee! That guy was a two-way lineman at Duke! His twin brother won the Outland Trophy, for heaven sakes! This was a big man. He has shrunk! He's wasted down to nothing!' Finally, somebody said, 'Coach, the Jerry McGee you're talking about, I think he's coaching high school ball. This guy isn't that guy.' I felt like such a dummy."

I tell Bobby Bowden not to feel too bad about it. I tell him it happens all the time and I even tell him the Ed Emory "Meet Mike McGee" story.

"Oh, I don't feel bad about it. Neither should your dad. Heck, I had dinner with my sons last week and I spent the whole night calling Terry, Tommy and calling Tommy, Terry. I'm just glad I didn't call up that other Jerry McGee to bless him out about a flag that your daddy threw on us."

CHAPTER 11

THE LONG GOODBYE

ONSIDERING THAT WE STARTED THIS BOOK with
Dad's final game and that game was played on January 8,
2009, then you've likely figured out that not only was the 2005
ACC Championship not the end of his officiating career, but
neither was the 2007 Rose Bowl between USC and Michigan...
or the 2008 Cotton Bowl between Missouri and Arkansas.

What we're saying is that "I think I'll do one more year"
became "I'm actually going to do three more years."

A big reason for that was Dad had a new sideline partner named Rick Page. Page's presence had reestablished that
crucial sixth sense–like trust that Dad had felt in the Booker
and McGee days. Page was funny, he loved the game, and his
mechanics were impeccable. So, the fun was back, though it
was admittedly a different kind of fun now.

The domino effect of money increasing stakes increasing
scrutiny increasing pressure was becoming overwhelming for
many coaches, and that scrutiny was spilling over into officiating as well. In fact, that '05 ACC Championship had resulted
in a meeting at the conference offices between the crew who
had worked the game and the Virginia Tech coaches. Frank

Beamer and the Hokies coaching staff had always been a cool-headed bunch, but they were convinced that they had lost a huge game in which they had been heavily favored because of the 17 penalty flags that had been thrown their way (Florida State was penalized a dozen times).

Dad

They had two huge turnovers in that game. They had two instances of 12 men on the field on punts, which gave the ball back to Florida State. They really struggled converting on third down (9 of 20). I think we found two plays we might have called differently.

But if you lose a big game like that, a game in which you were clearly the better team, who are you going to blame? Your play-calling? Your coaching staff that you hired? Your players whom you recruited? No way. You're going to blame seven strangers.

It was a pretty intense conversation, and it was a conversation that Coach Beamer and I continued to have a long time after that. Frank is one of my favorite people I've ever met in college football. He's just a good man. So, when he was that upset, it was big indicator to me about the increasing stress level for these guys.

The Internet, particularly social media, was also stripping away the anonymity that most officials had always held so dear. Ron Cherry, the white hat for most of Dad's biggest games in those final years, found himself accidentally famous during a 2007 NC State–Maryland game when he announced a penalty on TV, describing the personal foul as "Number 69 was giving him the business." It was actually a repeat of a description given by NFL referee Ben Drieth 20 years earlier, but YouTube didn't exist when Drieth was on the field. By day's end, some corners of Twitter were calling Cherry out for being a showboat, while others had created faux Twitter accounts claiming to be Cherry and posting smart-ass commentary on college games in the "giving him the business" style.

Websites and bloggers started tracking officials' game assignments and flags thrown in those games, seeking to detect patterns and habits. Instant replay moved into overdrive in 2006, and the ACC was among the pioneers in really pushing the use of video, including the establishment of a conference command center, where the coordinator could keep an eye on every game at once, instantly watching, clipping, and sending out any plays that might need a second look.

Dad

I always joke that the first time I used replay was a long time before that. We had a game in an NFL stadium that had a Jumbotron long before everyone had. We had a call on a turnover and there was a little bit of a question about exactly what happened, so we had a huddle on the field to discuss it.

I said to them, "You guys keep talking and don't pay attention to me, just act like I'm listening." While they did, I was nodding and everything, but I was really watching the replay on the Jumbotron. On the replay it was pretty clear what had happened, so I said, "Okay, we were right"....and we broke the huddle.

First down!

The assumption by many was that officials would resist replay, viewing it as some sort of Big Brother enemy designed for no reason other than to make them look bad, or a John Henry situation, where man was doomed to be replaced by machines. But in reality, they embraced it.

Okay, they embraced what it was in the beginning.

Dad

Our argument was that we would much rather stop the game on Saturday and get the call right than find out on Monday we had gotten it wrong. In my final years, replay was still pretty limited. We might have two stoppages of play per game and it was still being used only as a tool to get the call right. For me, plays on the sideline, on the goal line, catch or no catch, I wanted to get the call right just like I had always wanted to get it right. But I welcomed the help. As long as it remained that—help.

The clarity was great and so was the fact that replay really proved that we were right way more than we were wrong. People were really shocked that only a few calls needed to be overturned. But the never-ending scrutiny, that wasn't so great.

But we had a lot of conversations in those first years of replay with my fellow veteran officials about our fear of what the future might be for officiating. We could see a lot of young guys coming up raised on replay, and they were going to call the games like the NFL was doing with replay. If there was any question about catch or no catch, it was going to be a catch. Anytime it was a fumble or no fumble, it was a going to be a fumble. Because now they could go to replay and get it fixed.

Now what's happened is exactly what we were worried about. They do that, and you go to replay, but if there's not a good look, then you're stuck with what was called on the field. All of this, even though the guy on the field in his heart might think a play was out of bounds, but he called it inbounds so that they could get the help. But that help might not always be there. And when it's not, it's a mess.

Conversations like this became a big part of the enjoyment of those final three seasons, as the new young officials started rolling in. Doug Rhoads, Dad's old crewmate, hung up his whistle after 275 games worked and took over as the ACC officiating coordinator in 2007. Always a cutting-edge guy via his FBI training, Rhoads pushed video everywhere he could. He was never without his iPad, perpetually loaded with football plays about which he knew he was going to be questioned by coaches, media members, and his officials. He launched a website where those videos were available for review by his officials, day and night. He handed out his cell phone number to sportswriters and TV commentators and held regular Q&A sessions at conference events, eager to head off any would-be controversies by way of preemptive education.

With that same strategy in mind, Rhoads went to his old-school friends who were still on the field and asked them to embrace their mentorship roles. Dad certainly did.

Dad

What was cool was that even with all of the new technology there was to embrace, the lessons I tried to hand down to the young guys were exactly what I had been taught by my mentors, going all the way back to high school.

Dad would repeat the words of Mr. Allen Gaddy: "Timing is everything."

He would serve up the instructions of Mr. Cecil Longest: "Stay out the way. Play deep. Only call the obvious stuff. Learn all you can from the guys around you."

He would preach the lessons of Mr. Norval Neve: "Look through your play so you can anticipate what's happening," and, "Let your mind digest what your eyes have seen."

And he told the new guys what he had been told when he was the new guy, what Mr. W.C. Clary had always said: "Anybody in the stands could referee 95 percent of the plays that are going to happen here today. You're here to officiate the other five percent."

Sam

As a lawyer, I think about that last lesson every single time I am in a courthouse. That applies to being a field judge and it applies to being a judge in the courtroom. I will be sitting in a county courthouse tomorrow, and I will watch a lot of hearings before mine, and most of it will be easy. But mine will not, and the judge has to be ready to deal with mine as much as he is the easy stuff. That's the mark of anyone who has to make big decisions and do it on the spot. You can either handle those really difficult calls or you can't. Everyone thinks they can. But they aren't in that robe or in that officials' uniform, are they?

The summer after officiating in the January 1, 2008, Cotton Bowl, Dad also took another piece of advice that he had received from his mentors and called Doug Rhoads.

For all of the processes that college football officiating gets right, they are horrible at goodbyes. Now, they are really good about commemorating big moments, with watches and rings for big games and plaques honoring those who have hit milestones of 100, 200, 300 or more games worked.

But they fumbled retirements like a punt returner muffing an incoming kick. They loved officiating so much that they almost always hung on too long. They would get hurt or become slow and end up saddled with a schedule quality that was far beneath their glory days.

It was the officiating equivalent of Willie Mays falling down in the outfield in the 1973 World Series.

Dad

These were my heroes, and you would have to watch them on this decline.

It would put the supervisor in a hell of a difficult spot. They have to figure out a way to tell them that they are done. As gently as they know how, they have to say, "You have been so great for the game of college football. We appreciate you so much. I love you. But you're done."

There's no good way to handle that. Our supervisors would try to make it better by rewarding a veteran official with a bowl game, and then when that game was over, they'd walk into the locker room and say, "That was your last game." As well-intentioned as everyone was, nobody could get it right, and that created a lot of bitterness. I always wanted to see the veteran guys come to the rules clinic and have some beer and tell some stories and have a good time. I wanted them to still be in the family, but they would be so hurt about how they were shown the door that you couldn't get a lot of them to come back.

My closest friends on my crew, guys like Watts Key and Rick Page, I told them I was not going to let that happen. I also knew that Doug and I were so close that he was never going to tell me I was done, so I wanted to do that for him.

He told Rhoads he would be done at season's end. For real this time. In the history of the ACC, no football official had ever called the conference coordinator to say that they would be retiring. As of 2020, no one has done it since.

Sam

Neither Ryan nor I went to the Rose Bowl or Cotton Bowl in '07 and '08. We didn't think either one of those was going to be his last game. But when he was on the field at the Rose Bowl, I was in Miami because we were there to watch Wake Forest in the Orange Bowl. We were watching Dad on TV in a sports bar, and I had a moment of regret. I thought about his threat to intercept a pass and take off for the end zone.

Suddenly, I thought, maybe I should have gone, you know, just in case…

I had the same feeling during the Cotton Bowl one year later. I couldn't make it to Dallas because of work, but I was back home on New Year's Day. I had a moment of panic, suddenly scooping up my toddler daughter and posing her for a picture with Dad on TV in the background.

But in '08, with the bridge officially burned behind him at the ACC offices, we knew this would be it. At that summer's ACC clinic, everyone else knew it, too. Rhoads made the announcement to the officials.

The morning of the dreaded one-mile run, Dad experienced a genuine Hollywood sports movie moment. In the middle of his fourth and final lap, a group of the younger guys who had already finished spotted him. One of them ran out to meet him, ran alongside, and said, "You want some company?" Dad replied, "Absolutely. Misery loves company." Then another runner joined them. And another. And another. When Dad came to the finish line for his 27th timed-mile run as a Division I college football official, he was surrounded by a half-dozen younger colleagues.

He repaid that magical moment with a stunt worthy of the Booker and McGee Prank Hall of Fame.

Dad

We were having a big dinner in a really dark restaurant banquet room. Everyone had some drinks. I grabbed Mike Safirt, a second-generation ACC official. I'd worked games with his father and now with him. I told him I needed his help.

A few minutes later, I went to the front of the room and I dinged my glass with a spoon to get everyone's attention. I told them what a joy of my life it had been to be an official, the greatest fraternity in the world. I asked that they indulge me and allow me to give out some awards.

I would say like, "We all work so hard out here. You take a guy like Chris Brown back over there. He does it the right way. And that's why I'd like to give him this award..." He was a great official, and he was thrilled with the recognition. He came up and Mike handed him a trophy. It was beautiful. We gave out four of them. I thanked the room and said that I hoped they could find a special place for in their homes for their new awards. Then I said to Mike, "Let's get the hell out of here."

A little bit later, everyone else was leaving and the manager of the restaurant came running up. "What the hell do you guys think you're doing?!" They told him they'd had a great time and they showed him their trophies. "You can't have those! Those are ours!"

Mike and I had taken a bunch of "Restaurant of the Year" trophies from the front of the place. That's what we had given out.

It was a beautiful final season, and a busy one. When Duke and Georgia Tech met midseason, Dad caught himself getting a little emotional during the pregame. He was thinking about his very first college football game when he was 13, taken there by his daddy, Marshall Caddell. That game was Georgia Tech versus Duke, at that same stadium.

When a couple of ACC colleagues suffered injuries, Rhoads called Dad and asked him to step in. As a result, he worked the biggest schedule of his career in the final year of that career. That allowed him to hit nearly all of the old-school ACC stadiums and shake the hands of everyone he'd befriended since 1982. Stadium security guards, chain crews, ball boys, radio play-by-play announcers, equipment managers, trainers…all of the unsung heroes who keep college football running, all so important that they always outlast the higher-profile head coaches.

Sam

He had such a great year that I kept expecting him to say, "Hey, man, you know what, I might be walking away too early..." But he had already made his big announcement, and everywhere he went, people were saying goodbye.

Dad

Oh, there were definitely a couple of times where I thought, *Now, wait. Am I doing the right thing here?* But I was getting letters of congratulations from coaches. There were some sports columns written about me that fall. The *New York Times*; Furman Bisher wrote story in the *Atlanta Constitution Journal*. I started receiving letters from coaches all over the country, guys like Al Groh and Grant Teaff, the former Baylor head coach who was president of the American Football Coaches Association, and the ACC commissioner, John Swofford.

They were all saying, "Good for you, Jerry, you are really going out the right way."

Unfortunately, my plan had worked! The plan was too good. I couldn't back out now.

The only addition that could have promoted the plan from good to perfect was one more great bowl game. The only assignment missing from Dad's resume was the Sugar Bowl. He was in the San Antonio airport on business and chatting with a friend about wanting the Sugar Bowl when the phone rang from Doug Rhoads. He didn't the get Sugar Bowl. He had the BCS National Championship Game.

Yeah, the plan was now perfect.

I called my editor at *ESPN The Magazine*. "I don't know who you have assigned to cover the national title game and I don't care. They aren't going. I am. Also, I have a column idea of my own for the issue that comes out the week before: 'A tribute to my father..."' They said yes.

The game itself had a futuristic feel, with Urban Meyer's spread option offense versus an Oklahoma passing game that had averaged more than 50 points per game. These two teams playing for a national title meant that more and more teams around the nation would be leaning in to those types of offenses. This was a gateway game, a peek into the future and a testament to the single biggest change in the game that Dad had witnessed since his first Division I assignment more than 27 years earlier.

Dad

Speed, speed, and speed. The size of the players was obviously a big change, too. Now there were 300-pound linemen all over the field when we used to have maybe one. But even then, the more remarkable thing about those giants was how athletic they were, how fast they were.

When we were watching film and getting ready for that game, I thought about that evolution a lot. When I started calling college games, you knew what was going to happen. Everybody was going to run the ball on first and second down, throw a pass on third down, and punt on fourth down. Nobody could punt the ball more than 35 yards. We kicked it off from the 40-yard line and nobody could kick to the end zone. We might see one field goal a month.

These guys were running 70 offensive plays per game, and some were running 90. And back in the day you had a few guys on the field as fast Rocket Ismail and James Jett. These two teams looked like they were full of them.

If you had come to me at James Madison versus Virginia in 1982 and told me this is where college football would be by the time I was done, I would have thought you were nuts. What a gift to have witnessed that firsthand.

Amid all of that looking forward, there was also plenty of looking back. About two hours before kickoff, during the same pregame field walkthrough routine that had once created concerns about oak trees hanging the end zone and saplings-turned-first down markers, Dad called Coach Eutsler, now retired and living in rural South Carolina. They had the same conversation they always had when Dad inevitably checked in with his coach, from playing fields in South Bend and Happy Valley to Death Valley and Pasadena.

"Jerry," the coach said when he picked up the phone. "Where are you?"

"Coach, I'm on the 50-yard line at the national championship game."

"Well, shouldn't you be getting ready?!"

"Coach, I've been getting ready for this game my entire life."

He called Bill Booker. He wished he could have called Marshall Caddell, like he used to do, but Pa-Pa had been gone 10 years now. So, he called his brother and my brother to see if they were at the stadium yet.

Sam

I was so busy. I had a big legal conference in Raleigh the morning after the game, but there was no way I was missing this. I flew in late the afternoon of the game and I was scheduled to blow out of there at like 5:00 the morning after.

I think back now, and I was very nostalgic on the flight down and the flight back out, but not so much during the game. In the pregame, Danny and I got Dad's attention, but once it kicked off, I was so excited to be watching a national championship game in person, I really just went into game mode, like I always did.

I was in the auxiliary press box, almost directly above where Sam and Danny were sitting. In addition to my column that ran in *ESPN The Magazine* prior to the game, I had volunteered to pen a behind-the-scenes piece with the officiating crew. That morning I'd showed up for their film session and team discussion, walking in unannounced and sitting beside Dad, just like I had done so many times before at so many different ages. Only, this time I had a reporter's notebook and I was furiously scribbling down information that I could use in my story. I might have even had my laptop with me, hammering away at the keyboard as I snapped photos with my Blackberry.

Referee Ron Cherry shared some helpful hints he'd gathered from an officiating friend in the Big 12 who had seen Oklahoma's offense multiple times during the regular season. Ted Jackson, our old friend from church in Raleigh, was the replay official who would be in the press box, and he joined Dad in reminding the crew that it would be perfectly okay if a review took a beat longer than normal considering the stakes in the game. Dad said to the room, "No will remember tomorrow if we took 15 seconds to make sure we got a call right." Line judge Rich Misner and head linesman Sam Stephenson, the men guarding the line of scrimmage, warned the room that both teams run a lot of slip screens, which meant a lot of plays run right at them, so they said they might need a little extra backup when it came to watching their zones on those plays.

In the middle of the meeting, Doug Rhoads unleashed a vicious clip reel of the season's closest plays and most controversial penalties. This was by design. The officials hadn't had a game in a month and needed to shake off the rust. Plus, it was the biggest game in the world.

While the clips of sideline-straddling catches, horse-collar tackles, and fumble/no fumble played, Rhoads walked over and leaned in to whisper to me. "Um, you didn't by any chance clear this story with the ACC office, did you?"

I stopped typing and looked up at Mr. Rhoads. "No. I just showed up with Dad. He said it was cool."

"Okay," he replied, shaking his head. "What are we going to do now? Fire him?"

The game itself had so many moments when Dad couldn't help but tap into his lifetime with that access. His first tough call of the night came on Florida's first touchdown, when, not unlike Robbie Bosco in the '85 Citrus Bowl, quarterback Tim Tebow scrambled around on a busted play and spotted a receiver coming back toward him. It was Louis Murphy, who all at once caught the football and dove for the goal line as he was being wrapped up and slammed to the turf by a defender. His knee, body, and arm all hit the turf at once, and the ball was knocked loose. Dad paused for a beat. Touchdown, Florida.

Dad

In my final game, I was absolutely leaning on Mr. Neve's favorite lesson. "Let your mind digest what your eyes have just seen."

Dad was digesting again at the end of the first half when Sam Bradford hit an Oklahoma receiver in the hands at the goal line, but the ball popped out and was batted around like a hot rock between four different players, at one point coming perilously close to touching the turf and being blown dead. Again, Dad paused for a fraction of a second. Interception. Florida ball.

His third and final big call of the night came on one of those it-wasn't-this-fast-in-1982 plays. What looked like a long midfield reception by Oklahoma during what looked like the game-winning drive ended with a Florida interception from Ahmad Black. The defensive black flew into the area and snatched the ball from the hands of a Sooners receiver so quickly that only a super slow-motion replay revealed how he actually pulled it off, taking the ball from between the hands of the receiver as it ever-so-briefly bounced from his gloves during the would-be catch.

> ### Dad
>
> I looked at the back judge, Gary Patterson, and we were both like, "Did that really just happen?" But we had both seen it. We verified it. We signaled it. "Let your mind digest what your eyes have just seen."

In keeping with the full-circle theme of the night, this was the last time that Dad and Patterson would be sharing a field together, but it was not the first. That had happened way back in 1984, when Dad was still officiating a mix of ACC and small college games, and Patterson was a quarterback at Wofford.

The rest you know about from the beginning of this book. Me on the sideline for one last in-game chat. Dad running off the field, waving to Sam and Danny. The crew paying one more tribute. Tom Laverty showing off his Tim Tebow cleat marks. Dad wondering if he could wear his last uniform home.

Sam

I will say this. There was a moment—maybe it was after Ryan came down from the press box at halftime to say hello, maybe it was watching Dad out on the field, or maybe it was at the end. But a realization kind of came over me. I had chosen not to be a football official, and I didn't work for ESPN.

So...wait a minute...had I just lost my lifetime pass to college football games?!

I was in the press box very late. I finished my behind-the-scenes story, "A Day with the BCS Refs," and walked to my rental car. When I got to the hotel, I expected everyone to be in bed. Instead, I found Dad, Sam, Danny, and Marcella, whom Dad was marrying the very next weekend. Earlier, the other crewmates and their families had been there, but now only a few remained.

They were having beers and eating hotel pizza as SportsCenter showed the game highlights on the TVs above the bar, over and over again. When Danny saw me walking around the corner with my backpack, he shouted, "There he is! Come on and join us. Your Dad saw that Florida touchdown replay and now he knows for sure he got it right, so he is finally relaxed."

Sam

That had to have been, what, 2:00 or 3:00 AM? My taxi was picking me up for my flight in, like, two hours. I should have been in bed. But, whatever. As much I had always loved the games and the sideline passes and all of that, when I was a kid, this was the part that I think had the biggest impact on me. These grown-up guys, who had just been on the field for the game that everyone in town was there to see, they were letting me sit with them and hang out with them and listen to them break down the game.

Sometimes that was an uncomfortable conversation to listen to. I remember a game right there in that state, a game involving Florida, when Dad's crew had a couple of tough calls and the crowd had turned on them early, and the talk they had as a crew, it was so hard. But they had it. Because they cared that much. There were so many others, most of them, who were just the happiest group of guys you'd ever see in your life.

And they always let me sit there with them!

The next morning, Sam was gone to his conference. Danny and I were gone back to North Carolina. Dad and Marcella were leaving soon. But first, he had to stop by the BCS Championship souvenir stand in the lobby to buy a stack of ballcaps fashioned with the flashy game logo.

Dad

As soon as I got home, I drove to Rockingham and took hats to Ken Rankin and Jimmy Maske, the last of my old-school high school officiating friends. Then I drove to Coach Eutsler's. I told them all the same thing—that I wouldn't have been there if it hadn't been for them. Them and a lot of mentors and friends who were already gone.

I always did that, after every big bowl game I ever worked. All the way down to the last one.

Coach's Timeout
with Frank Beamer

"The last time you and I were at a game with these two teams, I wasn't super happy with your dad..."

It is Monday night, September 3, 2018, and Frank Beamer, the now-retired former Virginia Tech head coach, has just emerged from the tunnel at Florida State's Doak Campbell Stadium. I am there to do a Goodyear "Blimpcast" of the game with my ESPN colleague Marty Smith, but thanks to a tropical storm our ride has been grounded. Instead, we are on a tiny stage behind one end zone of the stadium, about to broadcast the game in a steady Tallahassee downpour. Beamer is there to support his old team. It has been nearly 13 years since the Hokies' loss to FSU in the inaugural ACC Championship, but he can't help but bring it up.

"I'm not mad at your dad anymore," the just-elected College Football Hall of Famer says with a handshake and a wink. "Even if I was, I'm too nice of a guy to tell you that."

Beamer is joking, because he is absolutely too nice of a guy to stay mad. Only a man as nice as Frank Beamer would be at the center of the story that he reminds me of next.

"Does your dad still have that football we sent him?"

The week before the 2009 BCS Championship, the Orange Bowl was also played at Dolphin Stadium, Beamer's ACC champion Hokies defeating the Big East champs from the University of Cincinnati. On the eve of that game, the two teams were at a dinner and, making small talk, Beamer asked the Orange Bowl executives what conference would be supplying the officials for the BCS title game the next week.

"When they told us it was the ACC, we all realized that was going to be your dad's crew, and we knew that was going to be his last game."

Beamer had his equipment manager retrieve a Virginia Tech–branded football. Then he explained to his feasting team who Dr. Jerry McGee was and why they should take a moment to honor him. Beamer had the ball passed around the room with a marker so that everyone on the roster could sign it. Then he handed the ball to the Orange Bowl brass.

"I told them to hang onto that football, make sure that Jerry McGee got it the next week, and to tell him that it was from his old Blacksburg friends from back in the Big East and the ACC."

There in Tallahassee a decade later, I tell Frank Beamer that the football is displayed prominently among Dad's college football collection. He does indeed beam.

"See?" he says, slapping me on the shoulder. "I told you I wasn't mad at him anymore."

CHAPTER 12

ZEBRA EMERITUS

THE MORNING AFTER DAD'S LAST GAME, I made the ultimate sportswriter misstep. I opened ESPN.com, clicked on my story "A Day with the BCS Refs," and scrolled down into the comments section. This was the first sentence that I read:

"OF COURSE THIS IDIOT WOULD WRITE SOMETHING NICE ABOUT THESE REFEREE IDIOTS. HIS LAST NAME IS THE SAME AS THE FIELD JUDGE. IT'S HIS DAMN DAD. REFS SUCK."

In the years since Dad's last game, I have written about him often. I have talked about him even more. I've done it so much that it has become a running joke with my ESPN college football coworkers. *"Hey, Ryan, your dad was a ref? Wow! You've never mentioned that!"*

But why wouldn't I? I now have the opportunity to cover college football, the very dream that was ignited on the sideline at Virginia in 1983, and my perspective on the game, which I believe to be unique, comes directly from my officiating bloodline. As a result, it will always be my ongoing mission to humanize officials, to try and help sports fans develop a better understanding of that third team on the field. People don't have to like officials. Most never will, and I know that. However, I honestly believe they can be smarter football fans if they have a better understanding of the men and women who blow their whistles not just on autumn weekends, but in every sport at every level.

Heck, that's why this book you currently hold in your hands exists!

Sam

I have seen firsthand that watching the officials in addition to the teams makes the game more interesting; I have seen that happen with my friends who started watching Dad because I made them. I know I probably drove them crazy with it in the beginning, but then one of them might say, "Man, your dad was all over that pass downfield," and that feels like a win.

But we aren't naïve here. We know there will always be way more people booing the officials or making fun of them than paying attention to them or respecting them, especially now.

In 2006, I wrote a two-page "Total Access" photo spread for *ESPN The Magazine*, taking a photographer behind the scenes with Dad's crew for a Maryland-Virginia game in Charlottesville. The experience was amazing. I was back on the sideline at UVA, not as a kid with my camera from Santa Claus, but with Les Stone, an award-winning, globe-trotting photographer who made his name as one of the planet's pre-eminent eyes for capturing the horrors of war. Les, attending his first college football game, had an incredible time as we watched Dad's crew meet, warm up, officiate a track meet of an offensive game, and then give Dad's old friend Clark Gaston the game ball for his 275th and final time on the field.

Les sent the images back to the magazine headquarters in New York. I was convinced this would be the kind of insider piece that would change the minds of millions of readers about the men they booed every Saturday. Then my editor called. I was sure he was going to heap praise upon me and tell me how I had forever altered his view of the men and women in stripes.

"Dude, we're going to lead with a big photo of two refs stretching their quads like they are about to play in the game or something. It's hilarious."

Dad

Down at Clemson one day, I was running off the field with Dr. Ernie Benson, a groundbreaking HBCU educator, and another official who was an attorney. Between us we had nine college degrees. This ol' boy in a Pabst Blue Ribbon hat who had about three teeth, he shook a beer at us and yelled, "Y'all's the three dumbest sumbitches ever been down here!"

You know what? We're probably never going to convince that guy that officials are actually pretty smart people who love football even more than he does. And that's okay.

But that doesn't mean we will stop trying.

Remember that "Hey Ref!" Q&A a few chapters back? For several years, Dad and I fielded questions from readers like that, and they seemed to like it. At that same time, I pitched a "Zebra Report" series for ESPN.com Insider, where I would call officials, many of whom I'd known for years and years, and they would give me "anonymous official" scouting reports on teams playing in big upcoming games. For example, a "Big East Head Linesman" provided a fantastic bit of info on West Virginia, then coached by Red Bull–guzzling, crazy-haired head coach Dana Holgorsen. The official explained there was always one stretch during every game when the WVU sideline would descend into chaos, with coaches yelling and players seemingly lost. He said that if an opponent were to recognize when that sideline inevitability was taking place, that window was the time to strike on offense.

Based on the reaction and page views, people seemed to really like that series. The teams, it turned out, didn't much care for it, particularly the folks in West by-god Virginia.

I believe the phone call from Doug Rhoads went something like this: "Ryan, Doug Rhoads here. I just left our national officiating coordinators meeting, and we talked about you for 45 minutes. Some coaches have complained about our guys talking to you about their guys. You know, I was a journalism major, so I love the idea. And we do look smart as hell. But you need to know that new regulations are being put into place stating that officials can no longer talk directly to the media without permission from the coordinators. So…good job."

That was almost a decade ago. Even now, I still run into officials in airports and they start laughing and running away from me. "No! I can't violate the Ryan McGee Rule!"

Dad

Yeah, Ryan got a little too specific on those. But the information was good. Otherwise, the coaches wouldn't have been so mad about it.

So, instead of aiming for mass audience officiating education, we are back to where we stared, trying to teach the public—and my press box colleagues—one officiating-hater at a time. And even though we can't be at games together very often, the game day text chains between me, Dad, and Sam remain a fall Saturday constant.

When I am covering a big college football game and there is a question about a downfield play—in or out of bounds, catch or no catch, pass interference or not—several of my fellow writers will instinctively look over to me and ask, "Well, what's your Dad say?" Within seconds, even without my asking, the text will arrive from Pops and I will announce to my row, "Dad says no way on that DPI!"

Sam

That's just how we watch football, and it will always be how we watch football.

One year, my alma mater, Wake Forest, made it to the Orange Bowl, and I took my wife down to Miami. Our seats were awful. If you ever see the huge Jumbotron in the upper deck at Dolphin Stadium, my back was resting up against that. We were as far away from the field as we could possibly be and still be inside the stadium.

Right before one play I started screaming from the top row, "Louisville has 12 men on the field! Louisville has 12 men on the field!" The flag was thrown and the PA announcer says, "Penalty, Louisville, substitution infraction, 12 men on the field."

I looked over at this guy who was staring at me. He said, "Wait, do you count the number of players on the field on every play?"

I said, "Of course I do. Don't you?"

To this point we've shared with you so many of the officiating questions Dad receives on a regular basis. But what about the question Sam and I hear the most? We get it from friends, from family, and we've always really gotten it from Dad's friends in stripes.

Why didn't we follow in Dad's cleat steps and become college football officials, too?

Sam

When I was a young man and grinding as a young attorney, people would ask me that question. I always said, "I have a very stressful job, the last thing I need is people yelling at me on the weekend." Or, "Why I would walk into a pressure cooker situation on the weekend? I'm already getting that all week."

My line always was, "Nobody yells at me when I'm fishing."

But here's the problem. Here's what I didn't get. The genius of this hobby for Dad was that it was a command performance. He had to be there. So, he could never say, "I'm too busy for my hobby."

Well, I have been too busy to fish most of my adult life. So, part of me says that if I had gone into officiating football when I was in my early twenties, like Dad did, it would have forced me to make sure that my hobby, something I was really passionate about, didn't get pushed to the side.

My wife, Marci, has told me before that I should have done it. I think she understands, like Ryan's wife, Erica, does, that we do have that real love for it.

Back in the day, Dad used to mention it every once in while. He felt like I could really see what happened on the field. And I know that was 100 percent because I was watching games through the lens of an official at a very early age.

Dad

We did talk about it. I always thought Sam had a tremendous sense of what was happening on the field. He had that ability to see the whole field. I think I knew that going all the way back to when he would be waiting for me when I got home from a game, with his sheet of paper and those three or four plays he questions about. But that's also how he made it into Yale Law and became an incredible attorney, because he approaches everything in his life like that.

I'm not disappointed that neither one of the boys became football officials. I'd say it's all worked out pretty well.

I never had that officiating conversation with Dad. Despite my deep appreciation for officiating, I never even considered doing it. From that very first time I snuck into the tower at Carter–Finley Stadium during an NC State scrimmage, it was the press box that was calling to me. Thankfully, my career path was established at a young age. It already had me fulfilling my childhood "How do I get paid to do this?!" sideline dreams.

Besides, if there were any doubts in my head as to whether or not I'd made the right football decision, they were silenced on March 31, 2018. That's when the SEC Network asked me to be the field judge in South Carolina's Garnet versus Black spring game.

There I was, on the same Williams-Brice Stadium sideline featured on Dad's Wall of Screaming. I wasn't receiving an earful from Joe Morrison or a face-in-the-hands reception from Lou Holtz. Instead, I had Gamecocks head coach Will Muschamp jawing at me. "We've got the wrong McGee out here! Where's your dad?!" Instead of me and Sam watching Dad on TV, they were watching me. Instead of me sitting in the stands with my Mom, my daughter Tara was there with her mom. And instead of Mom hoping her husband wouldn't be run over by an All-Conference linebacker, my wife, Erica, was the one doing the worrying.

Honestly, I thought it wasn't going to be that hard. I mean, c'mon, I'd been on sidelines since I was 13. I had always been there to shadow the field judge, and that was exactly the position that SEC officiating coordinator Steve Shaw made sure I was in now. How big of a difference could there really be standing on my regular side of the sideline as opposed to Dad's? What was it, six feet? It might as well have been half a mile. Only a few steps forward, onto the green grass, and I found that everything moved into warp speed.

I had one great moment, when recently retired head coach Steve Spurrier snuck onto the field to catch a pass from the South Carolina team, whom he'd been coaching the year before. But when the pass was behind him, the Head Ball Coach lost his footing and flopped right onto his back, the ball landing in the grass by his head. I ran over and asked, "Coach, you okay?" When he said yes, I pulled my flag off my belt and tossed it onto the turf next to him.

"What was that for?!" he asked me as he stood up and brushed himself off.

"That was for that bulls--t you yelled at my father during the '98 Citrus Bowl against Penn State!"

I also had one not-so-great moment. Okay, I had a few. But the big one was, naturally, a bang-bang touchdown catch right over the front corner end zone pylon, just like Dad's calls in the '97 Rose Bowl and '85 Citrus Bowl. The pass came right at me; the defender and receiver flew across my feet. I got totally turned around, and when I rallied, I realized that I had committed the ultimate field judge sin. I let the play get behind me. However, I was very proud of the fact that my feet were still in the right place, right on the goal line.

I signaled touchdown. Unfortunately, it was not a touchdown. Also, my feet were totally not at the goal line, as I had believed they were. They were at the 3-yard line. My real-life counterpart was Blake Parks, a longtime SEC field judge and a great guy. If I'd been paid a dollar for every time Blake had to say to me, "Back up!" or "No, straddle that goal line!" or "Get the spot, get the spot, get the spot!" I could have bought a skybox at Williams-Brice Stadium.

After the game, the sufficiently crusty SEC evaluator, NFL veteran Larry Rose, showed that play back to the entire crew, our ESPN media members as well as our SEC counterparts. He said, "Ryan McGee's father was as mechanically sound as anyone who has ever worn this uniform. But Ryan McGee made more positioning mistakes in one afternoon than his father made in the entire decade of the 1990s."

It was an insanely fun day. It was a dream come true. But if it's cool with y'all, I'm going to stay in my press box chair with my laptop, writing my words.

Sam

Ryan, how early do you get to the stadium when you are covering a game for ESPN?

I tell brother Sam that I walk into the gate as early as they will let me in there. Always.

Sam

Because that's the best part, right? Whether I was a ball boy at Furman or going somewhere with Dad, getting into the stadium before everyone else, that was the best part. It felt just like when I was playing baseball. The smell of the fresh-cut grass. The pregame radio show is playing on the loudspeakers. The stands are empty. You are a part of it. You feel like you are a part of the game.

Dad

Exactly. I had the same feeling then that I did when I played baseball. My cleats on the concrete. The music playing. It was like those John Philip Sousa marches over the loud-speaker in Rockingham.

Every time I officiated a game, from high school to Pasadena, we always did the same thing. We got to the stadium hours before kickoff and the first thing we did was put down our bags and say, "Let's go look at the field!"

We would walk around Death Valley at Clemson, and it would be 84,000 empty seats. There would be a couple of guys laying the lines for the sideline phones. The equipment guys would be setting up the bench area. Maybe someone was touching up the paint on the field just a little. There would be a half dozen people in the stadium, and us.

Then we would go into the locker room and get dressed, have a meeting, and when we came back out, now there are

> 84,000 people in there, and the bands are playing and the
> teams are warming up.
>
> It's crazy. It makes the hairs stand up my arm right now
> just talking about it.

The empty stadium conversation is taking place in the basement of my house in Charlotte. The table where we have just spent nearly two hours swapping stories is covered in empty pizza boxes, yellowed newspaper clippings (ACADEMIC MAKES CALLS ON, OFF FIELD), stacks of photos, and a couple of 30-year-old VHS tapes labeled in my teenaged handwriting.

We have retired to the television side of the room. I have YouTube fired back up and I'm riding the search bar. I dial up the 1985 Florida Citrus Bowl and find the touchdown play that still drives Dad nuts. Sam and I are comfortably reclined on couches, but Dad is on his feet, swaying back and forth. As the BYU receiver leaps toward the pylon past the outstretched arms of a Buckeyes defender, Dad leans in. The images are just as grainy as they were on our VCR in Raleigh, the play we watched and rewound over and over again. Like then, Dad is still sure he missed the call. And like then, Sam and I are still sure he got it right.

"You guys are mean, picking on your old man like this…"

Dad watches the film from '85 and starts talking about how much the game of college football changed during his years on the field. He talks about the Wishbone offense giving way to the Fun 'n' Gun and the Spread. He speaks of stadiums with crowds of 15,000 fans drawing crowds five times that size. Film into HDTV. Crews of five guys, hydrating with beer and steak, giving way to eight-man teams using eating and drinking processes prescribed by sports medicine specialists.

Officiating plays from six yards downfield...then 10...then 15...then 22...and 22 still didn't seem far enough to keep the quickening plays in front of you. Motel rooms full of chicken feathers in Jefferson City, Tennessee, to a palatial Fort Lauderdale resort on the eve of the national championship game. Bo Jackson, Charlie Ward, Julius Peppers, and Tim Tebow. Joe Paterno, Bobby Bowden, Danny Ford, Vince Dooley...

"Dan Henning!" Sam interjects.

"Dan Henning!" Dad and I shout back.

The McGee Boys are watching college football together. We are laughing and we are smiling.

You will never see us look happier than we are right now.

Just like Mom said.